The F2H-3/4 "Big Banjo" was the all-weather, high altitude outgrowth of the F2H-1/2 fighter series (see Naval Fighters #73). They were ordered under Contract Noa(s) 51-023 for 430 aircraft. It included 250 F2H-3s (BuNos 126291-126350, 126354-126489, and 127493-127546), 150 F2H-4s (126351-126353 and 127547-127693) and 30 F2H-2Ps. An additional order for 83 F2H-3/3Ps, BuNos 129050-129132, was cancelled.

To satisfy its mission the F2H-3/4 was required to be designed with a significant increase in range. To accomplish this the internal fuel capacity was more than doubled to 1,108 gallons through stretching the fuselage by 8 feet 1.6 inches to 48' 2". The fuel was carried in three tanks. The forward tank contained 512 gals., the center tank 184 gals., and the after tank contained 412 gals. The aircraft could carry an additional 340 gals. in two 170 gal. tip tanks if so fitted. Combat range for the F2H-3 without tip-tanks was 1,015 nautical miles and 1,490 with tip-tanks.

In addition to the fuselage extension, the tail surfaces of the F2H-3/4s were also redesigned. The horizontal tail was moved down to the rear of the fuselage tail cone and given a 10° dihedral. During service trials a tail flutter problem was encountered and a simple fix was developed. A dorsal extension was added to the horizontal tailplanes and retrofitted to most aircraft already in service. This extension was nothing more than a brace between the stabilizer and the fuselage with sheet aluminum riveted over it. The trailing edges of the wings were also extended on the F2H-3/4 series.

To accommodate the enlarged radar unit the four nose-mounted cannons were moved aft along the lower fuselage sides. Later in life, a refueling kit was developed and when installed the probe pipe replaced the upper left 20mm canon. A ventral fairing was also installed to cover additional external plumbing added with the refueling kit.

A F2H-2N, BuNo 123311, was used as the aerodynamic prototype for the series while still fitted with the F2H-2N nose as was F2H-2 BuNo 123204, which retained its original nose. First flight of the prototype was in December 1951.

The first production F2H-3 made its first flight on 29 March 1952. The F2H-4 series followed close on the heels of the -3 with F2H-3, BuNo 126319, being used as the prototype. Externally there was no difference

Above, the second F2H-3, BuNo 126292, in flight with a F2H-2P chase plane on 13 June 1952. (McDonnell)

between the two aircraft. Internally they carried two different types of radar. The F2H-3 utilized the Westinghouse APQ-41 radar with a 28" dish and the F2H-4 was equipped with the Hughes APG-37 radar. The F2H-4 further differed from the F2H-3 by having up-rated J34-WE-38 engines of 3,600 lb. thrust, an increase of 350 lb. thrust over the F2H-3's J34-WE-34 engine. The F2H-4's larger engines allowed for a service ceiling of 56,000 ft., which was 9,400 ft. greater than the -3 version, and a top speed of 610 mph versus 550 mph for the -3.

Wing stations were increased in the -3/-4 and the aircraft could carry either 8 100 lb. bombs, 8 250 lb. bombs, 2 500 lb. bombs, 8 5" HVAR rockets or 8 HPAG 5" rockets. Additionally, a large special weapons pylon could be fitted under the starboard wing. Furthermore, a Sidewinder kit was also produced to give the "Big Banjo" air-to-air capability. Because of the increase in weight from these weapons and clearance needed for a special weapon, the main gear was strengthened and a selectable nose gear extension was added.

Above, one of the F2H-3 aerodynamic prototypes seen on 20 December 1950 was created from F2H-2 BuNo 123204 by stretching the fuselage, adding a new tail and extending the wing chord. The original F2H-2 nose was retained. (Fred Roos collection) At left, F2H-2N BuNo 123311 was also used as an aerodynamic prototype for the F2H-3 and it retained its F2H-2N nose on its lengthened fuselage. Assigned to Tactical Test Division of NATC for testing, it has been fitted with afterburners. (USN) Below, F2H-2 and prototype F2H-3 (ex F2H-2N) comparison. (Fred Roos collection)

At top, McDonnell test pilot Chester Braun making the first take-off in the F2H-3 on 29 March 1952. (McDonnell) At right, F2H-3 BuNo 126301 seen from above giving a good view of the extended wing trailing edge inboard of the fold and original tailplane before the dorsal extension. (NMNA) Above, F2H-3 BuNo 126301 on 21 August 1953. (NMNA) Below, first production F2H-3 BuNo 126291 test fitted with Sparrow I missiles. (NMNA)

Above, public relations photo of a gloss sea blue F2H-3 in front of the factory at St. Louis. (McDonnell) Below, F2H-4 at St. Louis with the special weapons pylon installed and a TX-8 nuclear shape fitted for weapons carriage tests. The nose wheel is in the extended position. (McDonnell)

F2H-4

Above, F2H-4 BuNo 127556 on take-off from the McDonnell factory in 1953. Radome was black and weapons pylons were gloss sea blue. (USMC) At left, the last Banshee built was delivered on 24 September 1953. It was F2H-4 BuNo 127693. Below, excellent belly view of F2H-4 BuNo 126344. Although listed as a -3, 126344 was completed as a F2H-4. (USMC)

Above, landing gear drop testing being done on a "Big Banjo". (McDonnell) Below, F2H-3/4, TV-1, F3D rework line at NAS North Island, CA, in 1954. (USN via Rich Dan)

1954

OPERATING LIMITATIONS

AIRSPEED LIMITATIONS:

FLAP EXTENSION	165 Knots IAS
FLAP RETRACTION	174 Knots IAS
LANDING GEAR EXTENSION	174 Knots IAS
LANDING GEAR RETRACTION	174 Knots IAS
ARRESTING GEAR EXTENSION	225 Knots IAS
CANOPY OPENING	570 Knots IAS
CANOPY CLOSING	300 Knots IAS
SPEED BRAKE OPENING	570 Knots IAS
DIVING	570 Knots IAS
UNRESTRICTED USE OF AILERONS	399 Knots IAS
WITH FULL TIP TANKS	400 Knots IAS
	or .8 Mach
	whichever is less

ENGINE LIMITATIONS:

A. Normal engine operation should not exceed 100%

B. When operating engines without mixers above 30,000 ft. do not exceed 96% (12,000 rpm) Note, this restriction was removed with mixers installed

C. Turbine outlet temperature limits during starting:
960°C for the first five seconds of acceleration
793°C after the five seconds of starting to idle rpm

D. Turbine outlet temperature limits during acceleration from idle to military power: Advance throttles rapidly from idle to military power. If acceleration to military is not reached in 15 seconds, shut down engine and investigate the cause. During acceleration the turbine outlet temperature should not exceed:
960°C for the first five seconds of acceleration
793°C for the balance of the acceleration

E. Maximum normal turbine outlet temperatures were:
With mixers	650°C
Without mixers	682°C

PROHIBITED MANEUVERS:

A. Avoid extended inverted flight involving negative Gs

B. Maneuvers at sea level
Without pitching acceleration	7.5G limit
	-3,0G limit
Rolling pull-outs	6.0G limit
	1-1,0G limit

C. Maneuvers at 20,000 feet or above
Acceleration without pitching	7.0G limit
	-3.0G limit
Rolling pull-outs	6.0G limit
	-1.0G limit

D. Maneuvers in excess of 4.5Gs with tip tanks full

E. Maneuvers with 500 lb bombs on the outer panels

F. Arrested landings with 500 lb bombs on the outer panels

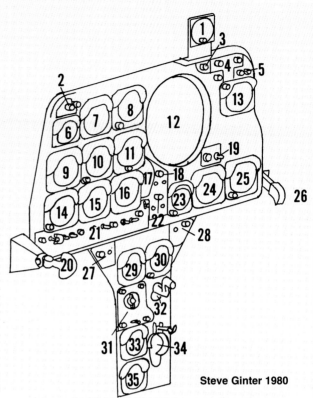

Steve Ginter 1980

F2H-3 INSTRUMENT PANEL

1. STANDBY COMPASS
2. ALTITUDE LOW LIMIT INDICATOR
3. L. ENG. FIRE WARNING LIGHT
4. FIRE WARNING TEST SWITCHES
5. R. ENG. FIRE WARNING LIGHT
6. ANGLE OF ATTACK INDICATOR
7. TACHOMETER INDICATOR
8. RADIO ALTIMETER INDICATOR
9. AIRSPEED INDICATOR
10. MASTER DIRECTION INDICATOR
11. GYRO HORIZON INDICATOR
12. RADAR FLIGHT INDICATOR
13. RADIO COMPASS INDICATOR
14. ALTIMETER
15. TURN AND BANK INDICATOR
16. RATE-OF-CLIMB INDICATOR
17. GYRO HORIZON SWITCH AND WARNING LIGHT
18. OIL PRESSURE INDICATORS
19. COMPASS SWITCH
20. LANDING GEAR CONTROL HANDLE
21. ARMAMENT CONTROL PANEL
22. OIL TEMPERATURE INDICATORS
23. CLOCK
24. FUEL QUANTITY INDICATOR
25. FUEL FLOW TOTALIZER INDICATOR
26. ARRESTING GEAR CONTROL HANDLE
27. L. TIP TANK AUX. FUEL FLOW INDICATOR
28. R. TIP TANK AUX. FUEL FLOW INDICATOR
29. TURBINE OUTLET TEMPERATURE INDICATOR
30. ACCELEROMETER
31. BOMB & ROCKET STATION SELECTOR &
PNEUMATIC COMPRESSOR SWITCH
32. RUDDER PEDAL ADJ. CRANK
33. PNEUMATIC PRESSURE GAUGE
34. RELIEF TUBE STOWAGE
35. HYDRAULIC PRESSURE GAUGE

F2H-3/4 COCKPIT GENERAL ARRANGEMENT

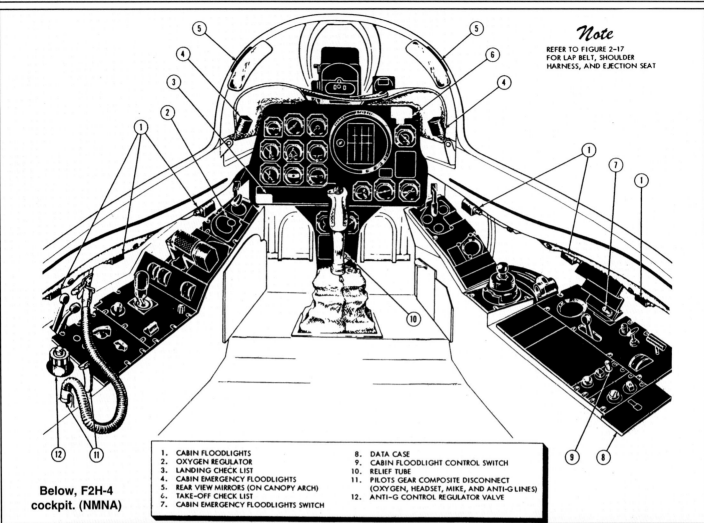

Note
REFER TO FIGURE 2-17
FOR LAP BELT, SHOULDER
HARNESS, AND EJECTION SEAT

1.	CABIN FLOODLIGHTS	8.	DATA CASE
2.	OXYGEN REGULATOR	9.	CABIN FLOODLIGHT CONTROL SWITCH
3.	LANDING CHECK LIST	10.	RELIEF TUBE
4.	CABIN EMERGENCY FLOODLIGHTS	11.	PILOTS GEAR COMPOSITE DISCONNECT
5.	REAR VIEW MIRRORS (ON CANOPY ARCH)		(OXYGEN, HEADSET, MIKE, AND ANTI-G LINES)
6.	TAKE-OFF CHECK LIST	12.	ANTI-G CONTROL REGULATOR VALVE
7.	CABIN EMERGENCY FLOODLIGHTS SWITCH		

**Below, F2H-4
cockpit. (NMNA)**

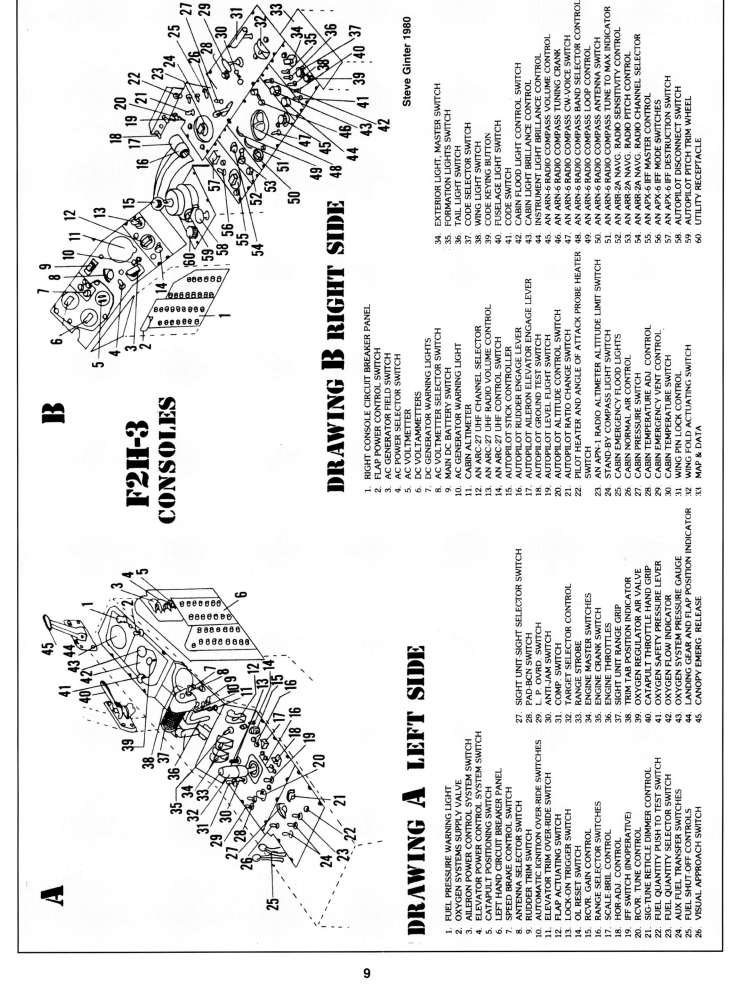

A

B

F2H-3 CONSOLES

Steve Ginter 1980

DRAWING A LEFT SIDE

1. FUEL PRESSURE WARNING LIGHT
2. OXYGEN SYSTEMS SUPPLY VALVE
3. AILERON POWER CONTROL SYSTEM SWITCH
4. ELEVATOR POWER CONTROL SYSTEM SWITCH
5. CATAPULT POSITIONING SWITCH
6. LEFT HAND CIRCUIT BREAKER PANEL
7. SPEED BRAKE CONTROL SWITCH
8. ANTENNA SELECTOR SWITCH
9. RUDDER TRIM SWITCH
10. AUTOMATIC IGNITION OVER-RIDE SWITCHES
11. ELEVATOR TRIM OVER-RIDE SWITCH
12. FLAP ACTUATING SWITCH
13. LOCK-ON TRIGGER SWITCH
14. OL RESET SWITCH
15. RCVR. GAIN CONTROL
16. RANGE SELECTOR SWITCHES
17. SCALE-BRIL CONTROL
18. HOR-ADJ. CONTROL
19. IFF SWITCH (INOPERATIVE)
20. RCVR. TUNE CONTROL
21. SIG-TUNE RETICLE DIMMER CONTROL
22. FUEL QUANTITY PUSH TO TEST SWITCH
23. FUEL QUANTITY SELECTOR SWITCH
24. AUX FUEL TRANSFER SWITCHES
25. FUEL SHUT-OFF CONTROLS
26. VISUAL APPROACH SWITCH
27. SIGHT UNIT -SIGHT SELECTOR SWITCH
28. PAD-BCN SWITCH
29. L. P. OVRD. SWITCH
30. ANTI-JAM SWITCH
31. COMP. SWITCH
32. TARGET SELECTOR CONTROL
33. RANGE STROBE
34. ENGINE MASTER SWITCHES
35. ENGINE CRANK SWITCH
36. ENGINE THROTTLES
37. SIGHT UNIT RANGE GRIP
38. TRIM TAB POSITION INDICATOR
39. OXYGEN REGULATOR AIR VALVE
40. CATAPULT THROTTLE HAND GRIP
41. OXYGEN SAFETY PRESSURE LEVER
42. OXYGEN FLOW INDICATOR
43. OXYGEN SYSTEM PRESSURE GAUGE
44. LANDING GEAR AND FLAP POSITION INDICATOR
45. CANOPY EMERG. RELEASE

DRAWING B RIGHT SIDE

1. RIGHT CONSOLE CIRCUIT BREAKER PANEL
2. FLAP POWER CONTROL SWITCH
3. AC GENERATOR FIELD SWITCH
4. AC POWER SELECTOR SWITCH
5. AC VOLTMETER
6. DC VOLTAMMETERS
7. DC GENERATOR WARNING LIGHTS
8. AC VOLTMETER SELECTOR SWITCH
9. MAIN DC BATTERY SWITCH
10. AC GENERATOR WARNING LIGHT
11. CABIN ALTIMETER
12. AN ARC-27 UHF CHANNEL SELECTOR
13. AN ARC-27 UHF RADIO VOLUME CONTROL
14. AN ARC-27 UHF CONTROL SWITCH
15. AUTOPILOT STICK CONTROLLER
16. AUTOPILOT RUDDER ENGAGE LEVER
17. AUTOPILOT AILERON ELEVATOR ENGAGE LEVER
18. AUTOPILOT GROUND TEST SWITCH
19. AUTOPILOT LEVEL FLIGHT SWITCH
20. AUTOPILOT ALTITUDE CONTROL SWITCH
21. AUTOPILOT RATIO CHANGE SWITCH
22. PILOT HEATER AND ANGLE OF ATTACK PROBE HEATER
    SWITCH
23. AN APN-1 RADIO ALTIMETER ALTITUDE LIMIT SWITCH
24. STAND-BY COMPASS LIGHT SWITCH
25. CABIN EMERGENCY FLOOD LIGHTS
26. CABIN NORMAL AIR CONTROL
27. CABIN PRESSURE SWITCH
28. CABIN TEMPERATURE ADJ. CONTROL
29. CABIN EMERGENCY VENT CONTROL.
30. CABIN TEMPERATURE SWITCH
31. WING PIN LOCK CONTROL
32. WING FOLD ACTUATING SWITCH
33. MAP & DATA
34. EXTERIOR LIGHT, MASTER SWITCH
35. FORMATION LIGHTS SWITCH
36. TAIL LIGHT SWITCH
37. CODE SELECTOR SWITCH
38. WING LIGHT SWITCH
39. CODE KEYING BUTTON
40. FUSELAGE LIGHT SWITCH
41. CODE SWITCH
42. CABIN FLOOD LIGHT CONTROL SWITCH
43. CABIN LIGHT BRILLANCE CONTROL
44. INSTRUMENT LIGHT BRILLANCE CONTROL
45. AN ARN-6 RADIO COMPASS VOLUME CONTROL
46. AN ARN-6 RADIO COMPASS TUNING CRANK
47. AN ARN-6 RADIO COMPASS CW-VOICE SWITCH
48. AN ARN-6 RADIO COMPASS BAND SELECTOR CONTROL
49. AN ARN-6 RADIO COMPASS LOOP CONTROL
50. AN ARN-6 RADIO COMPASS ANTENNA SWITCH
51. AN ARN-6 RADIO COMPASS TUNE TO MAX INDICATOR
52. AN ARR-2A NAVG. RADIO SENSITIVITY CONTROL
53. AN ARR-2A NAVG. RADIO PITCH CONTROL
54. AN ARR-2A NAVG. RADIO CHANNEL SELECTOR
55. AN APX-6 IFF MASTER CONTROL
56. AN APX-6 IFF MODE SWITCHES
57. AN APX-6 IFF DESTRUCTION SWITCH
58. AUTOPILOT DISCONNECT SWITCH
59. AUTOPILOT PITCH TRIM WHEEL
60. UTILITY RECEPTACLE

McDONNELL F2H-4 LEFT - HAND CONSOLE

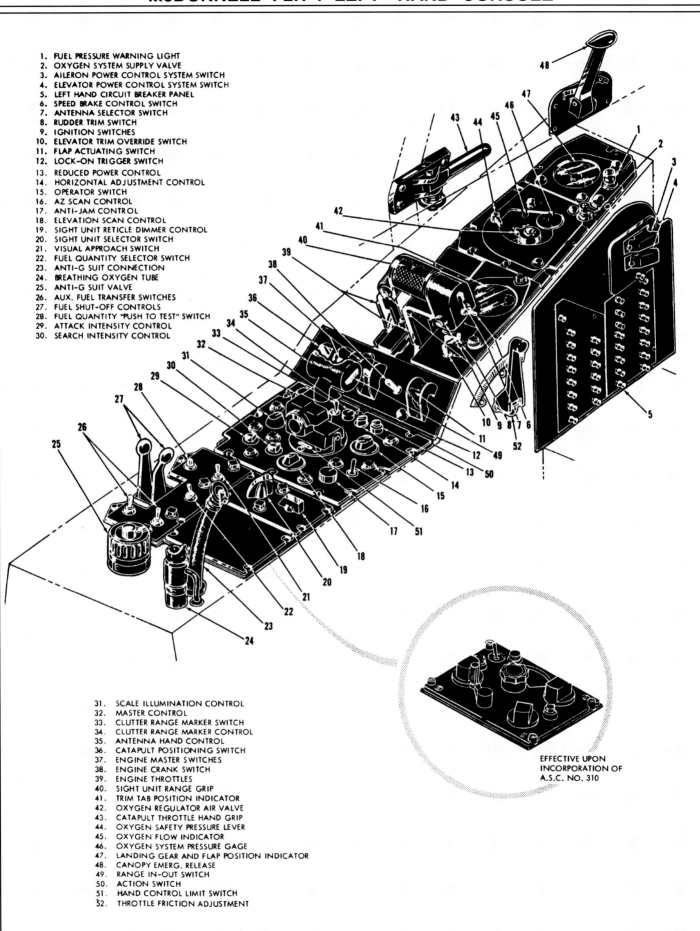

1. FUEL PRESSURE WARNING LIGHT
2. OXYGEN SYSTEM SUPPLY VALVE
3. AILERON POWER CONTROL SYSTEM SWITCH
4. ELEVATOR POWER CONTROL SYSTEM SWITCH
5. LEFT HAND CIRCUIT BREAKER PANEL
6. SPEED BRAKE CONTROL SWITCH
7. ANTENNA SELECTOR SWITCH
8. RUDDER TRIM SWITCH
9. IGNITION SWITCHES
10. ELEVATOR TRIM OVERRIDE SWITCH
11. FLAP ACTUATING SWITCH
12. LOCK-ON TRIGGER SWITCH
13. REDUCED POWER CONTROL
14. HORIZONTAL ADJUSTMENT CONTROL
15. OPERATOR SWITCH
16. AZ SCAN CONTROL
17. ANTI-JAM CONTROL
18. ELEVATION SCAN CONTROL
19. SIGHT UNIT RETICLE DIMMER CONTROL
20. SIGHT UNIT SELECTOR SWITCH
21. VISUAL APPROACH SWITCH
22. FUEL QUANTITY SELECTOR SWITCH
23. ANTI-G SUIT CONNECTION
24. BREATHING OXYGEN TUBE
25. ANTI-G SUIT VALVE
26. AUX. FUEL TRANSFER SWITCHES
27. FUEL SHUT-OFF CONTROLS
28. FUEL QUANTITY "PUSH TO TEST" SWITCH
29. ATTACK INTENSITY CONTROL
30. SEARCH INTENSITY CONTROL

31. SCALE ILLUMINATION CONTROL
32. MASTER CONTROL
33. CLUTTER RANGE MARKER SWITCH
34. CLUTTER RANGE MARKER CONTROL
35. ANTENNA HAND CONTROL
36. CATAPULT POSITIONING SWITCH
37. ENGINE MASTER SWITCHES
38. ENGINE CRANK SWITCH
39. ENGINE THROTTLES
40. SIGHT UNIT RANGE GRIP
41. TRIM TAB POSITION INDICATOR
42. OXYGEN REGULATOR AIR VALVE
43. CATAPULT THROTTLE HAND GRIP
44. OXYGEN SAFETY PRESSURE LEVER
45. OXYGEN FLOW INDICATOR
46. OXYGEN SYSTEM PRESSURE GAGE
47. LANDING GEAR AND FLAP POSITION INDICATOR
48. CANOPY EMERG. RELEASE
49. RANGE IN-OUT SWITCH
50. ACTION SWITCH
51. HAND CONTROL LIMIT SWITCH
52. THROTTLE FRICTION ADJUSTMENT

EFFECTIVE UPON
INCORPORATION OF
A.S.C. NO. 310

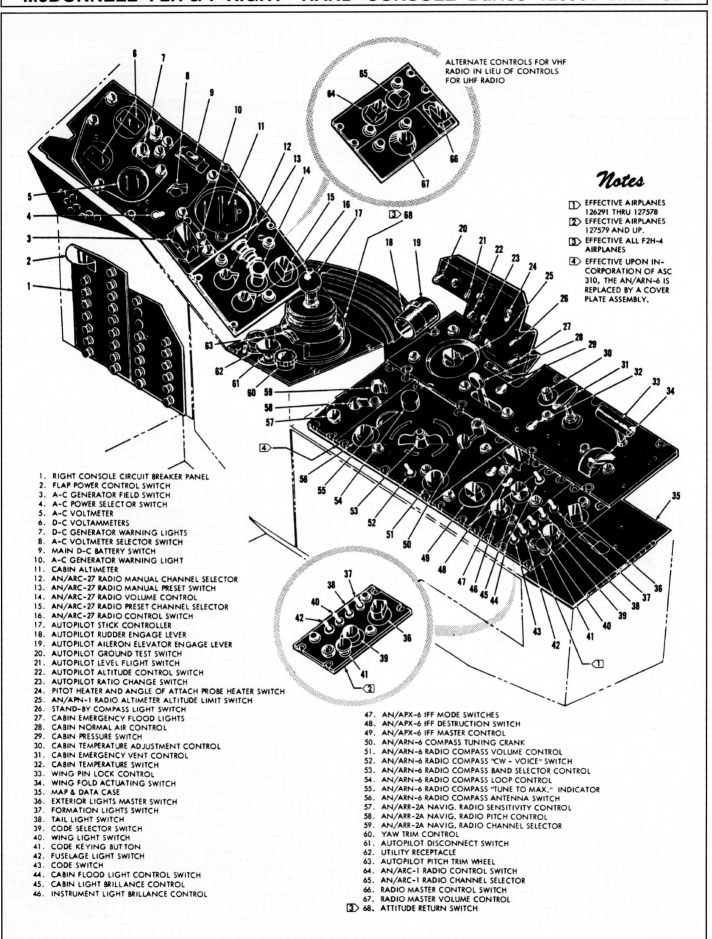

ALTERNATE CONTROLS FOR VHF
RADIO IN LIEU OF CONTROLS
FOR UHF RADIO

Notes

1▷ EFFECTIVE AIRPLANES
126291 THRU 127578

2▷ EFFECTIVE AIRPLANES
127579 AND UP.

3▷ EFFECTIVE ALL F2H-4
AIRPLANES

4▷ EFFECTIVE UPON IN-
CORPORATION OF ASC
310, THE AN/ARN-6 IS
REPLACED BY A COVER
PLATE ASSEMBLY.

1. RIGHT CONSOLE CIRCUIT BREAKER PANEL
2. FLAP POWER CONTROL SWITCH
3. A-C GENERATOR FIELD SWITCH
4. A-C POWER SELECTOR SWITCH
5. A-C VOLTMETER
6. D-C VOLTAMMETERS
7. D-C GENERATOR WARNING LIGHTS
8. A-C VOLTMETER SELECTOR SWITCH
9. MAIN D-C BATTERY SWITCH
10. A-C GENERATOR WARNING LIGHT
11. CABIN ALTIMETER
12. AN/ARC-27 RADIO MANUAL CHANNEL SELECTOR
13. AN/ARC-27 RADIO MANUAL PRESET SWITCH
14. AN/ARC-27 RADIO VOLUME CONTROL
15. AN/ARC-27 RADIO PRESET CHANNEL SELECTOR
16. AN/ARC-27 RADIO CONTROL SWITCH
17. AUTOPILOT STICK CONTROLLER
18. AUTOPILOT RUDDER ENGAGE LEVER
19. AUTOPILOT AILERON ELEVATOR ENGAGE LEVER
20. AUTOPILOT GROUND TEST SWITCH
21. AUTOPILOT LEVEL FLIGHT SWITCH
22. AUTOPILOT ALTITUDE CONTROL SWITCH
23. AUTOPILOT RATIO CHANGE SWITCH
24. PITOT HEATER AND ANGLE OF ATTACH PROBE HEATER SWITCH
25. AN/APN-1 RADIO ALTIMETER ALTITUDE LIMIT SWITCH
26. STAND-BY COMPASS LIGHT SWITCH
27. CABIN EMERGENCY FLOOD LIGHTS
28. CABIN NORMAL AIR CONTROL
29. CABIN PRESSURE SWITCH
30. CABIN TEMPERATURE ADJUSTMENT CONTROL
31. CABIN EMERGENCY VENT CONTROL
32. CABIN TEMPERATURE SWITCH
33. WING PIN LOCK CONTROL
34. WING FOLD ACTUATING SWITCH
35. MAP & DATA CASE
36. EXTERIOR LIGHTS MASTER SWITCH
37. FORMATION LIGHTS SWITCH
38. TAIL LIGHT SWITCH
39. CODE SELECTOR SWITCH
40. WING LIGHT SWITCH
41. CODE KEYING BUTTON
42. FUSELAGE LIGHT SWITCH
43. CODE SWITCH
44. CABIN FLOOD LIGHT CONTROL SWITCH
45. CABIN LIGHT BRILLANCE CONTROL
46. INSTRUMENT LIGHT BRILLANCE CONTROL

47. AN/APX-6 IFF MODE SWITCHES
48. AN/APX-6 IFF DESTRUCTION SWITCH
49. AN/APX-6 IFF MASTER CONTROL
50. AN/ARN-6 COMPASS TUNING CRANK
51. AN/ARN-6 RADIO COMPASS VOLUME CONTROL
52. AN/ARN-6 RADIO COMPASS "CW - VOICE" SWITCH
53. AN/ARN-6 RADIO COMPASS BAND SELECTOR CONTROL
54. AN/ARN-6 RADIO COMPASS LOOP CONTROL
55. AN/ARN-6 RADIO COMPASS "TUNE TO MAX." INDICATOR
56. AN/ARN-6 RADIO COMPASS ANTENNA SWITCH
57. AN/ARR-2A NAVIG. RADIO SENSITIVITY CONTROL
58. AN/ARR-2A NAVIG. RADIO PITCH CONTROL
59. AN/ARR-2A NAVIG. RADIO CHANNEL SELECTOR
60. YAW TRIM CONTROL
61. AUTOPILOT DISCONNECT SWITCH
62. UTILITY RECEPTACLE
63. AUTOPILOT PITCH TRIM WHEEL
64. AN/ARC-1 RADIO CONTROL SWITCH
65. AN/ARC-1 RADIO CHANNEL SELECTOR
66. RADIO MASTER CONTROL SWITCH
67. RADIO MASTER VOLUME CONTROL
3▷ 68. ATTITUDE RETURN SWITCH

McDONNELL F2H-3/4 EJECTION SEAT

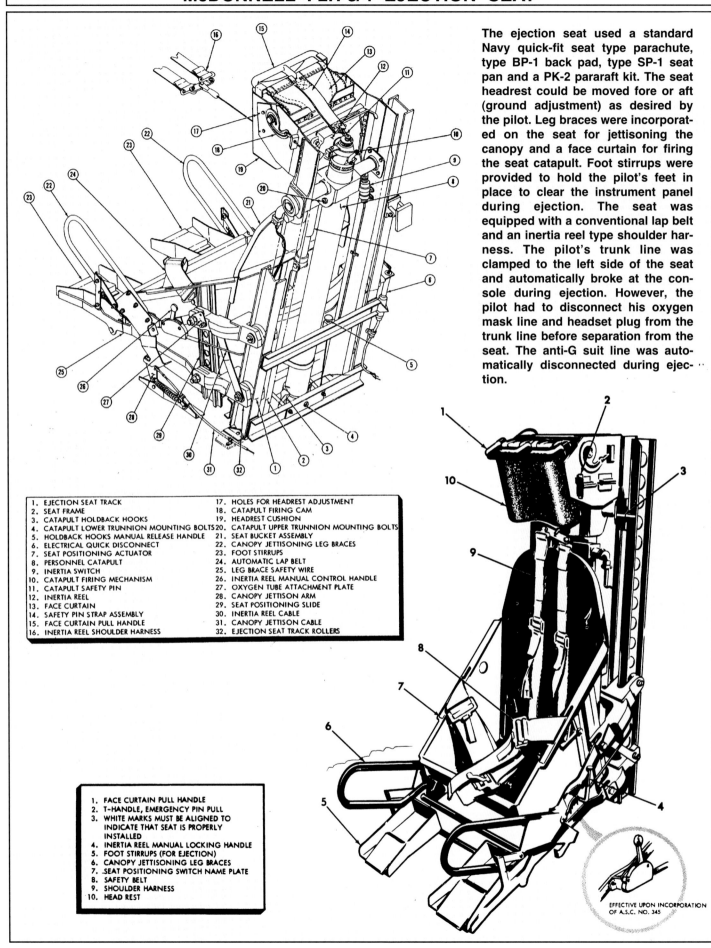

The ejection seat used a standard Navy quick-fit seat type parachute, type BP-1 back pad, type SP-1 seat pan and a PK-2 pararaft kit. The seat headrest could be moved fore or aft (ground adjustment) as desired by the pilot. Leg braces were incorporated on the seat for jettisoning the canopy and a face curtain for firing the seat catapult. Foot stirrups were provided to hold the pilot's feet in place to clear the instrument panel during ejection. The seat was equipped with a conventional lap belt and an inertia reel type shoulder harness. The pilot's trunk line was clamped to the left side of the seat and automatically broke at the console during ejection. However, the pilot had to disconnect his oxygen mask line and headset plug from the trunk line before separation from the seat. The anti-G suit line was automatically disconnected during ejection.

1. EJECTION SEAT TRACK
2. SEAT FRAME
3. CATAPULT HOLDBACK HOOKS
4. CATAPULT LOWER TRUNNION MOUNTING BOLTS
5. HOLDBACK HOOKS MANUAL RELEASE HANDLE
6. ELECTRICAL QUICK DISCONNECT
7. SEAT POSITIONING ACTUATOR
8. PERSONNEL CATAPULT
9. INERTIA SWITCH
10. CATAPULT FIRING MECHANISM
11. CATAPULT SAFETY PIN
12. INERTIA REEL
13. FACE CURTAIN
14. SAFETY PIN STRAP ASSEMBLY
15. FACE CURTAIN PULL HANDLE
16. INERTIA REEL SHOULDER HARNESS

17. HOLES FOR HEADREST ADJUSTMENT
18. CATAPULT FIRING CAM
19. HEADREST CUSHION
20. CATAPULT UPPER TRUNNION MOUNTING BOLTS
21. SEAT BUCKET ASSEMBLY
22. CANOPY JETTISONING LEG BRACES
23. FOOT STIRRUPS
24. AUTOMATIC LAP BELT
25. LEG BRACE SAFETY WIRE
26. INERTIA REEL MANUAL CONTROL HANDLE
27. OXYGEN TUBE ATTACHMENT PLATE
28. CANOPY JETTISON ARM
29. SEAT POSITIONING SLIDE
30. INERTIA REEL CABLE
31. CANOPY JETTISON CABLE
32. EJECTION SEAT TRACK ROLLERS

1. FACE CURTAIN PULL HANDLE
2. T-HANDLE, EMERGENCY PIN PULL
3. WHITE MARKS MUST BE ALIGNED TO INDICATE THAT SEAT IS PROPERLY INSTALLED
4. INERTIA REEL MANUAL LOCKING HANDLE
5. FOOT STIRRUPS (FOR EJECTION)
6. CANOPY JETTISONING LEG BRACES
7. SEAT POSITIONING SWITCH NAME PLATE
8. SAFETY BELT
9. SHOULDER HARNESS
10. HEAD REST

EFFECTIVE UPON INCORPORATION OF A.S.C. NO. 345

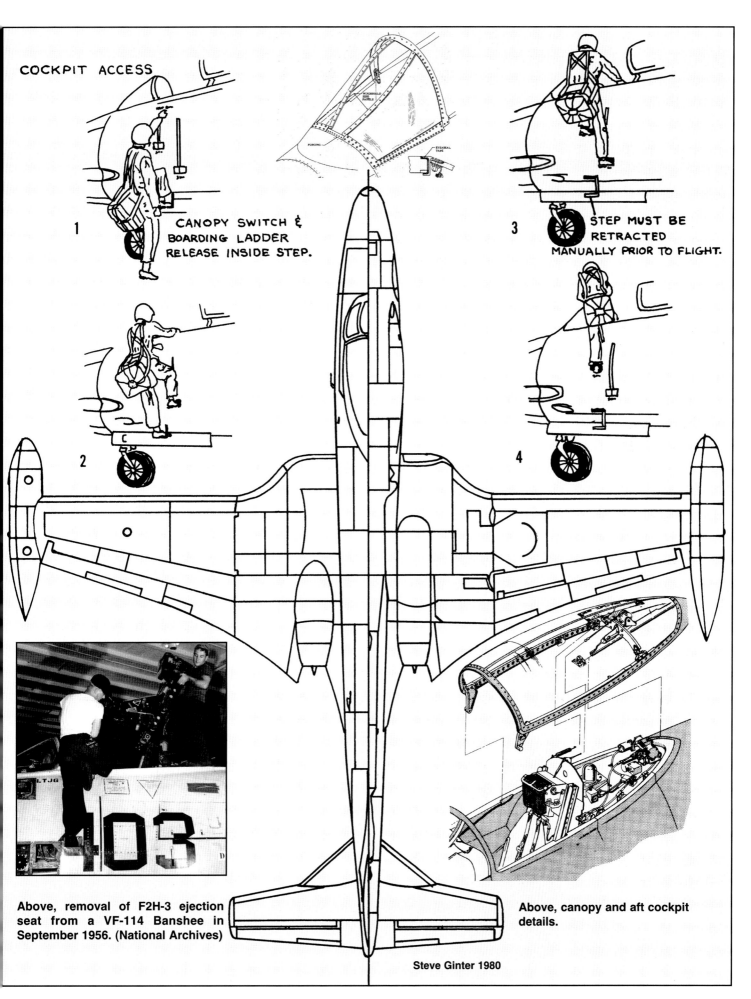

COCKPIT ACCESS

1 — CANOPY SWITCH & BOARDING LADDER RELEASE INSIDE STEP.

2

3 — STEP MUST BE RETRACTED MANUALLY PRIOR TO FLIGHT.

4

Above, removal of F2H-3 ejection seat from a VF-114 Banshee in September 1956. (National Archives)

Above, canopy and aft cockpit details.

Steve Ginter 1980

13

INDEX NO.	NOMENCLATURE	FIGURE NO.
1	Battery	27
2	Plug – Battery	70
3	Unit – Angle of Attack Relay	70
4	Unit – Rate and Accelerometer	70
5	Circuit Breaker – Remote Control Compressor	70
6	Panel Assembly – Relay	70
7	Switch – Air Speed Pressure	70
8	Plugs – Quick Disconnect	30, 31
9	Receptacles – Quick Disconnect	75
10	Regulator – Cabin Pressure	52
11	Thermostat – Cabin Air	52
12	Box – Cabin Control	52
13	Panel Assembly – RH Console Circuit Breaker	62
14	Control – Auto Pilot Engagement	62
15	Controller – Auto Pilot	62
16	Link Assembly – Yaw Damper Force	43
17	Detector – Air Stream Direction	33
18	Controller – Gunsight	71
19	Regulator – Voltage	71
20	Box Assembly – Cockpit Electrical	71
21	Switch – Canopy Close Limit	71
22	Panel Assembly – Canopy Electrical	71
23	Resistor Assembly – Interior Lights	71
24	Box – Gunsight Relay	71
25	Motor – Canopy Actuating	96
26	Switch – Canopy	77
27	Vibrator – Stall Warning	42
28	Grip Assembly – Control Stick	42
29	Switch – Arresting Gear Control	69
30	Switch – Landing Gear Control	69
31	Valve Assembly – Catapult Launching	55
32	Valve – Pneumatic Solenoid	55
33	Pedestal – Instrument	65
34	Panel Assembly – Main Instrument	64
35	Gunsight – MK 8 MOD O	67
36	Panel Assembly – Switch	57
37	Panel Assembly – RH Aft Circuit Breaker	34
38	Actuator Assembly – Nose Landing Gear Retracting	48

INDEX NO.	NOMENCLATURE	FIGURE NO.
39	Panel Assembly – Left Hand Console Circuit Breaker	58
40	Quadrant – Engine Power	58
41	Unit – Aileron Servo	45
42	Valve – Air Flow & Temperature Control	53
43	Unit Assembly – Refrigeration	53
44	Heater – Gun	75
45	Trigger – Electric	75
46	Valve – Pneumatic Solenoid	120
47	Valve – Gun Charger	120
48	Regulator – Absolute Pressure Pneumatic	120
49	Compressor – Air	120
50	Pump – Fuel Transfer	152
51	Unit Assembly – Fueling and Defueling	152
52	Unit – Forward Cell Gaging	152
53	Pump – Fuel	153
54	Unit – Center Cell Gaging	153
55	Switch Assembly – Fuselage Cell Transfer	153
56	Tee – Fuel Cell Gage & Float Switch	157
57	Cable Assembly – Fuel Cell	157
58	Switch – Fuel Pressure	151
59	Indicator – Wing Tip Tank Fuel Flow	92
60	Transmitter – Autosyn Fuel Flow	112
61	Unit – Aft Cell Gaging	154
62	Unit Assembly – Fuel & Defueling	154
63	Pump – Fuel Transfer	154
64	Actuator – Flap	89
65	Light Assembly – Lower Fuselage Door	94
66	Light Assembly – Upper Fuselage Door	97
67	Camera – Gun	130

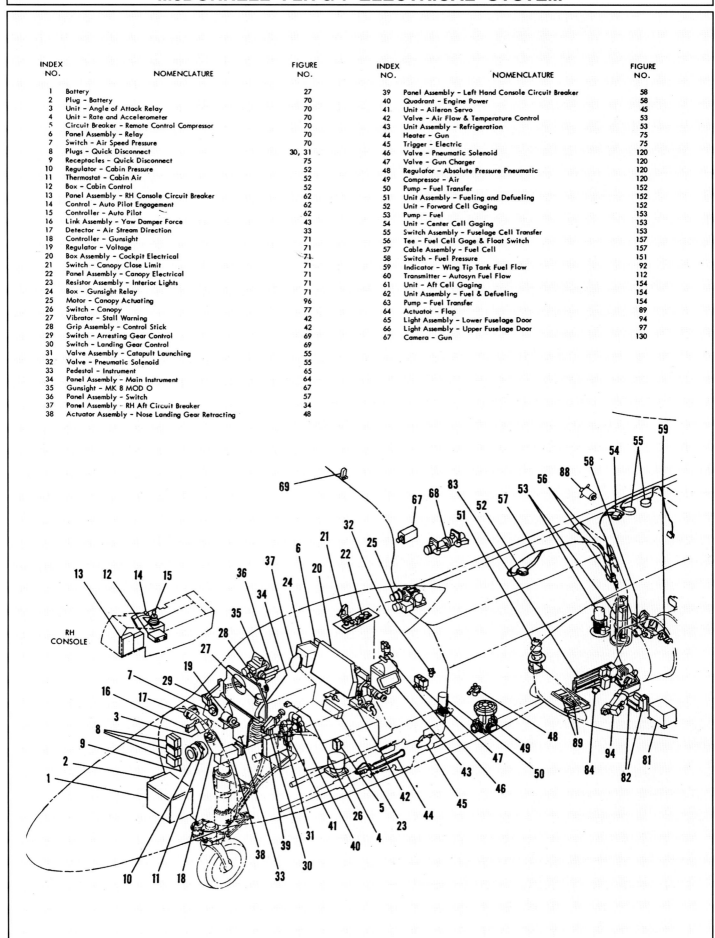

RH CONSOLE

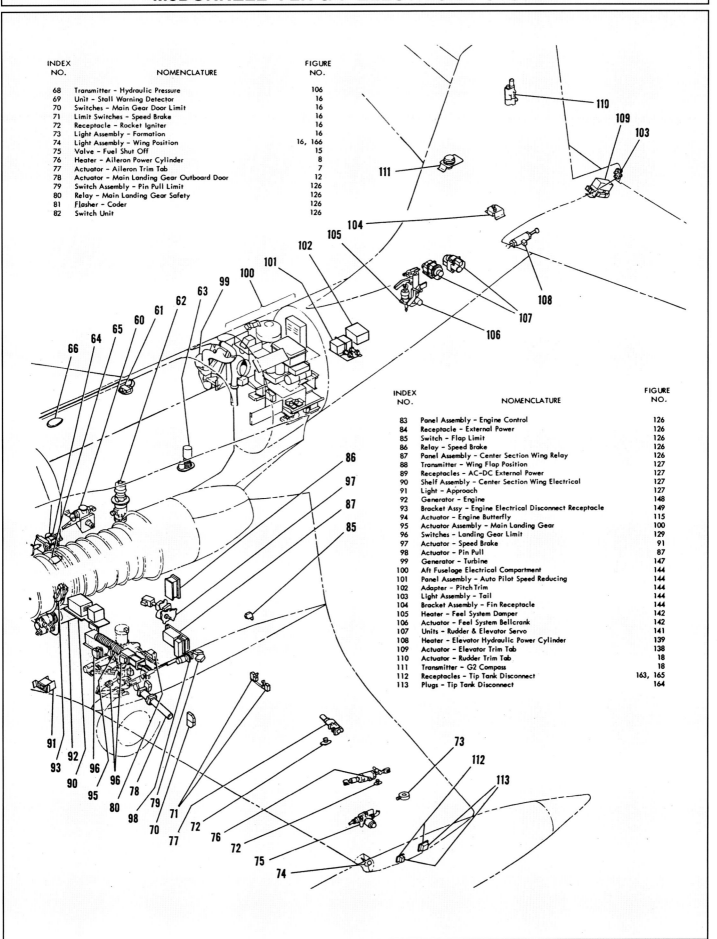

INDEX NO.	NOMENCLATURE	FIGURE NO.
68	Transmitter – Hydraulic Pressure	106
69	Unit – Stall Warning Detector	16
70	Switches – Main Gear Door Limit	16
71	Limit Switches – Speed Brake	16
72	Receptacle – Rocket Igniter	16
73	Light Assembly – Formation	16
74	Light Assembly – Wing Position	16, 166
75	Valve – Fuel Shut Off	15
76	Heater – Aileron Power Cylinder	8
77	Actuator – Aileron Trim Tab	7
78	Actuator – Main Landing Gear Outboard Door	12
79	Switch Assembly – Pin Pull Limit	126
80	Relay – Main Landing Gear Safety	126
81	Flasher – Coder	126
82	Switch Unit	126

INDEX NO.	NOMENCLATURE	FIGURE NO.
83	Panel Assembly – Engine Control	126
84	Receptacle – External Power	126
85	Switch – Flap Limit	126
86	Relay – Speed Brake	126
87	Panel Assembly – Center Section Wing Relay	126
88	Transmitter – Wing Flap Position	127
89	Receptacles – AC-DC External Power	127
90	Shelf Assembly – Center Section Wing Electrical	127
91	Light – Approach	127
92	Generator – Engine	148
93	Bracket Assy – Engine Electrical Disconnect Receptacle	149
94	Actuator – Engine Butterfly	115
95	Actuator Assembly – Main Landing Gear	100
96	Switches – Landing Gear Limit	129
97	Actuator – Speed Brake	91
98	Actuator – Pin Pull	87
99	Generator – Turbine	147
100	Aft Fuselage Electrical Compartment	144
101	Panel Assembly – Auto Pilot Speed Reducing	144
102	Adapter – Pitch Trim	144
103	Light Assembly – Tail	144
104	Bracket Assembly – Fin Receptacle	144
105	Heater – Feel System Damper	142
106	Actuator – Feel System Bellcrank	142
107	Units – Rudder & Elevator Servo	141
108	Heater – Elevator Hydraulic Power Cylinder	139
109	Actuator – Elevator Trim Tab	138
110	Actuator – Rudder Trim Tab	18
111	Transmitter – G2 Compass	18
112	Receptacles – Tip Tank Disconnect	163, 165
113	Plugs – Tip Tank Disconnect	164

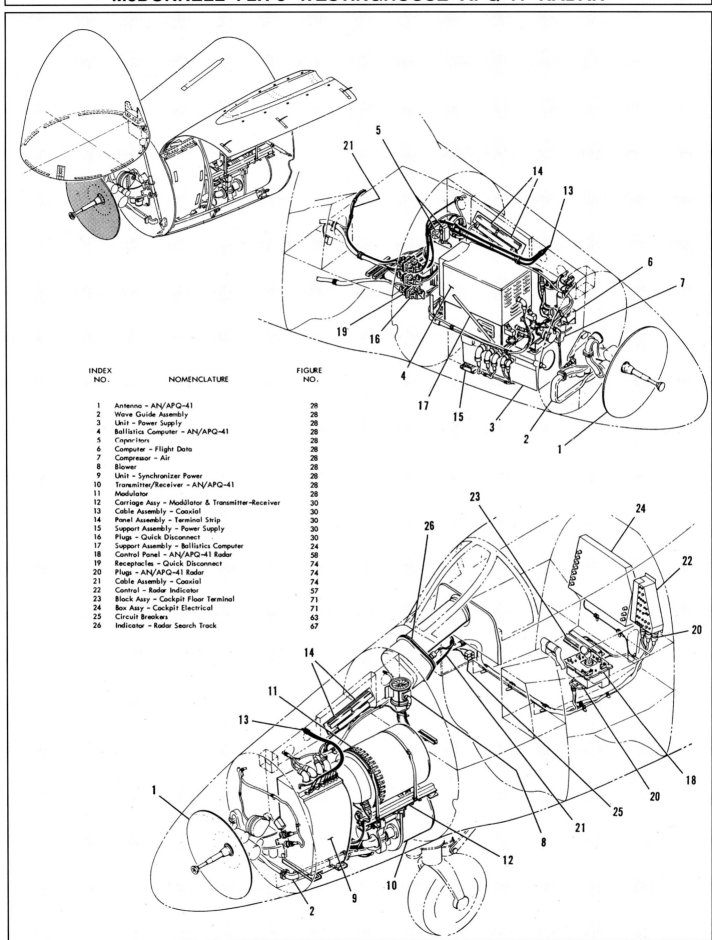

INDEX NO.	NOMENCLATURE	FIGURE NO.
1	Antenna – AN/APQ-41	28
2	Wave Guide Assembly	28
3	Unit – Power Supply	28
4	Ballistics Computer – AN/APQ-41	28
5	Capacitors	28
6	Computer – Flight Data	28
7	Compressor – Air	28
8	Blower	28
9	Unit – Synchronizer Power	28
10	Transmitter/Receiver – AN/APQ-41	28
11	Modulator	28
12	Carriage Assy – Modulator & Transmitter-Receiver	30
13	Cable Assembly – Coaxial	30
14	Panel Assembly – Terminal Strip	30
15	Support Assembly – Power Supply	30
16	Plugs – Quick Disconnect	30
17	Support Assembly – Ballistics Computer	24
18	Control Panel – AN/APQ-41 Radar	58
19	Receptacles – Quick Disconnect	74
20	Plugs – AN/APQ-41 Radar	74
21	Cable Assembly – Coaxial	74
22	Control – Radar Indicator	57
23	Block Assy – Cockpit Floor Terminal	71
24	Box Assy – Cockpit Electrical	71
25	Circuit Breakers	63
26	Indicator – Radar Search Track	67

The Westinghouse APQ-41 in the F2H-3 was not as user friendly as that of the F2H-4. The Hughes APG-37 system provided a stabilized horizon line. The Westinghouse unit's scan banked with a turn. More importantly, the Hughes system could lock on a selected target and provide a steering dot. Three search ranges were provided on the Hughes system: 200 miles, 100 miles and 10 miles

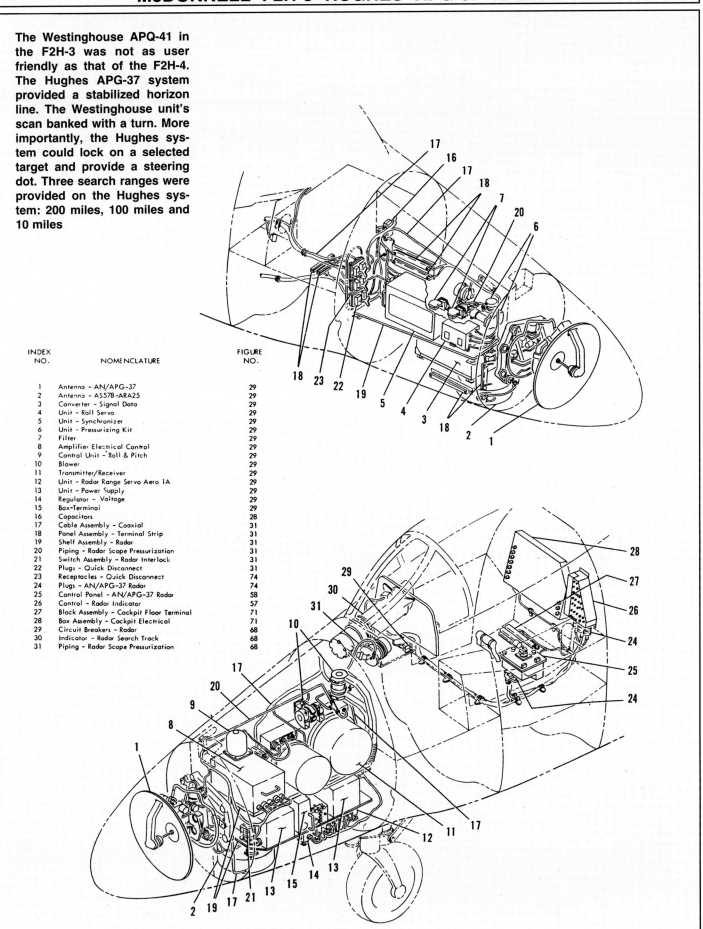

INDEX NO.	NOMENCLATURE	FIGURE NO.
1	Antenna – AN/APG-37	29
2	Antenna – AS578-ARA25	29
3	Converter – Signal Data	29
4	Unit – Roll Servo	29
5	Unit – Synchronizer	29
6	Unit – Pressurizing Kit	29
7	Filter	29
8	Amplifier Electrical Control	29
9	Control Unit – Roll & Pitch	29
10	Blower	29
11	Transmitter/Receiver	29
12	Unit – Radar Range Servo Aero 1A	29
13	Unit – Power Supply	29
14	Regulator – Voltage	29
15	Box-Terminal	29
16	Capacitors	28
17	Cable Assembly – Coaxial	31
18	Panel Assembly – Terminal Strip	31
19	Shelf Assembly – Radar	31
20	Piping – Radar Scope Pressurization	31
21	Switch Assembly – Radar Interlock	31
22	Plugs – Quick Disconnect	31
23	Receptacles – Quick Disconnect	74
24	Plugs – AN/APG-37 Radar	74
25	Control Panel – AN/APG-37 Radar	58
26	Control – Radar Indicator	57
27	Block Assembly – Cockpit Floor Terminal	71
28	Box Assembly – Cockpit Electrical	71
29	Circuit Breakers – Radar	68
30	Indicator – Radar Search Track	68
31	Piping – Radar Scope Pressurization	68

At left, maintenance of a Hughes F2H-4 radar unit on a VMF-214 Banshee aboard the USS Hancock (CVA-19) in May 1957. (National Archives)

Below, the installation of the Hughes radar system (APG-37) in a F2H-4 on 28 July 1953 at Hughes in California. F2H-3/4 radomes were either tan (at left) or black as seen here. (Hughes via Paul Freiler)

18

McDONNELL F2H-3/4 FOUR 20mm GUN SYSTEM

The aircraft was equipped with four fixed, forward-firing 20mm cannon. The guns were located on the outboard sides of the forward fuselage, two on each side. Ammo was supplied to each gun from two ammunition boxes located above the guns. The guns were equipped with pneumatic feeders and chargers and electric triggers. Expended links and cases were forced into a compartment inboard of the guns and removed after flight. Armament controls were incorporated on the lower left side of the main instrument panel. The controls consisted of the armament MASTER switch and two GUN CONTROL switches. The gun trigger switch was integral with the control stick. Each gun was equipped with a thermostatically controlled heater. A gun camera mounted in the leading edge of the right wing was incorporated into the firing circuit and operated whenever the guns were fired.

Above, VMF-214 F2H-4 on CVA-19 in May 1957 being loaded with ammo and bombs. (National Archives)

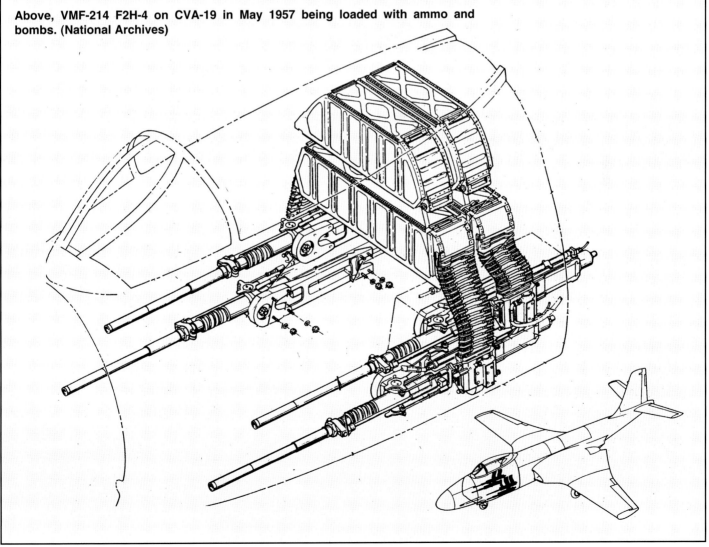

McDONNELL F2H-3/4 CONVENTIONAL WEAPONS

LOCATION (STATION)	ROCKETS		100LB. BOMBS
	HVAR	HPAG	
4 5	X	X	X
3 6	X	X	X
2 7	X	X	X
1 8	X	X	X

250LB. BOMBS	500LB. BOMBS	LOW DRAG 500LB. BOMBS	
		NON CAT	CAT
X	X	X	X
X	X	X	X
X	X	X	
X	X	X	

Steve Ginter 1980

8   7   6 5   4 3   2   1

Bomb and Rocket Equipment: This airplane was equipped with 8 Aero 14A rocket launchers and bomb racks. These were located on the lower sides of the wings. The racks are designed to carry rockets and up to 500 lb bombs. The racks were operated electrically and controlled by the pilot in the cockpit.

Bomb and Rocket Controls: The controls for both the bombs and rockets were located on the armament panel on the lower left side of the main instrument panel. The station selector was located on the pedestal panel. The electric controls consisted of the armament MASTER switch, with ON and OFF positions, bomb and rocket control switch with SAFE and READY positions and bomb and

rocket arming switch with NOSE and TAIL, SAFE, and TAIL positions. The fire control selector switch with GUNS and 5" HVAR positions, dive angle switch with 35° and over and 35° and under positions, and the Mk. 2 Mod 0 station selector. The bomb and rocket release button was located on the control stick handle.

Firing Order: The station selector was an eight-position switch, which controlled the firing order and release of the bombs. Stations were 1-2-3-4 for singles, and 5-6-7-8 for pairs. As the bomb and rocket release button was pressed it advanced automatically to the next station until all the bombs or rockets were fired. The pointer could be rotated counterclockwise and the bombs were dropped

and the rockets were fired in the following order:

FIRING ORDER - SINGLES

Station Selector Position	Launcher Station
1	1
2	7
3	3
4	5
5	8
6	2
7	6
8	4

FIRING ORDER - PAIRS

Station Selector Position	Launcher Station
5	1/8
6	2/7
7	3/6
8	4/5

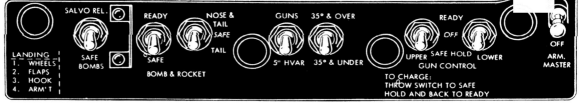

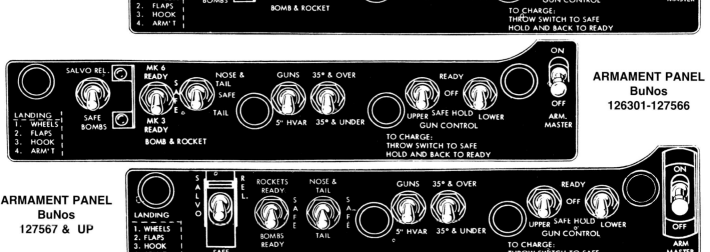

ARMAMENT PANEL
BuNos
126291-126300

ARMAMENT PANEL
BuNos
126301-127566

ARMAMENT PANEL
BuNos
127567 & UP

McDONNELL F2H-3 CONVENTIONAL WEAPONS LOADING

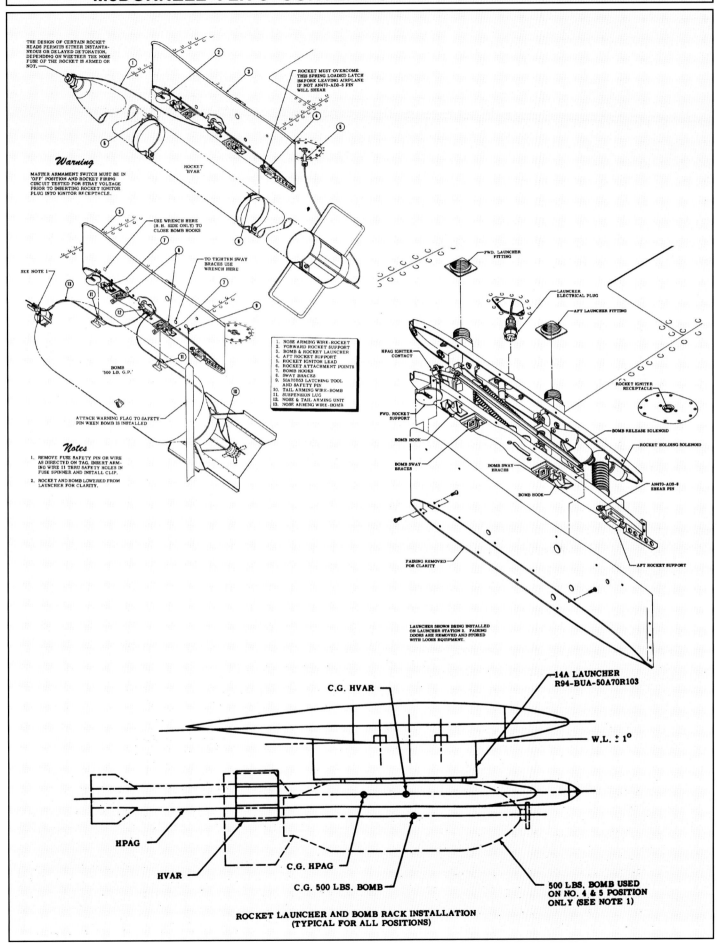

THE DESIGN OF CERTAIN ROCKET HEADS PERMITS EITHER INSTANTANEOUS OR DELAYED DETONATION, DEPENDING ON WHETHER THE NOSE FUSE OF THE ROCKET IS ARMED OR NOT.

ROCKET MUST OVERCOME THIS SPRING LOADED LATCH BEFORE LEAVING AIRPLANE IF NOT AN470-AD3-8 PIN WILL SHEAR

ROCKET 'HVAR'

Warning

MASTER ARMAMENT SWITCH MUST BE IN 'OFF' POSITION AND ROCKET FIRING CIRCUIT TESTED FOR STRAY VOLTAGE PRIOR TO INSERTING ROCKET IGNITOR PLUG INTO IGNITOR RECEPTACLE.

USE WRENCH HERE (R. H. SIDE ONLY) TO CLOSE BOMB HOOKS

TO TIGHTEN SWAY BRACES USE WRENCH HERE

SEE NOTE 1

BOMB '500 LB. G.P.'

ATTACH WARNING FLAG TO SAFETY PIN WHEN BOMB IS INSTALLED

1. NOSE ARMING WIRE-ROCKET
2. FORWARD ROCKET SUPPORT
3. BOMB & ROCKET LAUNCHER
4. AFT ROCKET SUPPORT
5. ROCKET IGNITOR LEAD
6. ROCKET ATTACHMENT POINTS
7. BOMB HOOKS
8. SWAY BRACES
9. 50A70B53 LATCHING TOOL AND SAFETY PIN
10. TAIL ARMING WIRE-BOMB
11. SUSPENSION LUG
12. NOSE & TAIL ARMING UNIT
13. NOSE ARMING WIRE-BOMB

Notes

1. REMOVE FUSE SAFETY PIN OR WIRE AS DIRECTED ON TAG. INSERT ARMING WIRE 11 THRU SAFETY HOLES IN FUSE SPINNER AND INSTALL CLIP.

2. ROCKET AND BOMB LOWERED FROM LAUNCHER FOR CLARITY.

FWD. LAUNCHER FITTING

LAUNCHER ELECTRICAL PLUG

AFT LAUNCHER FITTING

HPAG IGNITER CONTACT

FWD. ROCKET SUPPORT

ROCKET IGNITER RECEPTACLE

BOMB HOOK

BOMB SWAY BRACES

BOMB SWAY BRACES

BOMB HOOK

BOMB RELEASE SOLENOID

ROCKET HOLDING SOLENOID

AN470-AD3-8 SHEAR PIN

AFT ROCKET SUPPORT

FAIRING REMOVED FOR CLARITY

LAUNCHER SHOWN BEING INSTALLED ON LAUNCHER STATION 3. FAIRING DOORS ARE REMOVED AND STORED WITH LOOSE EQUIPMENT.

C.G. HVAR

14A LAUNCHER R94-BUA-50A70R103

W.L. ± 1°

HPAG

HVAR

C.G. HPAG

C.G. 500 LBS. BOMB

500 LBS. BOMB USED ON NO. 4 & 5 POSITION ONLY (SEE NOTE 1)

ROCKET LAUNCHER AND BOMB RACK INSTALLATION (TYPICAL FOR ALL POSITIONS)

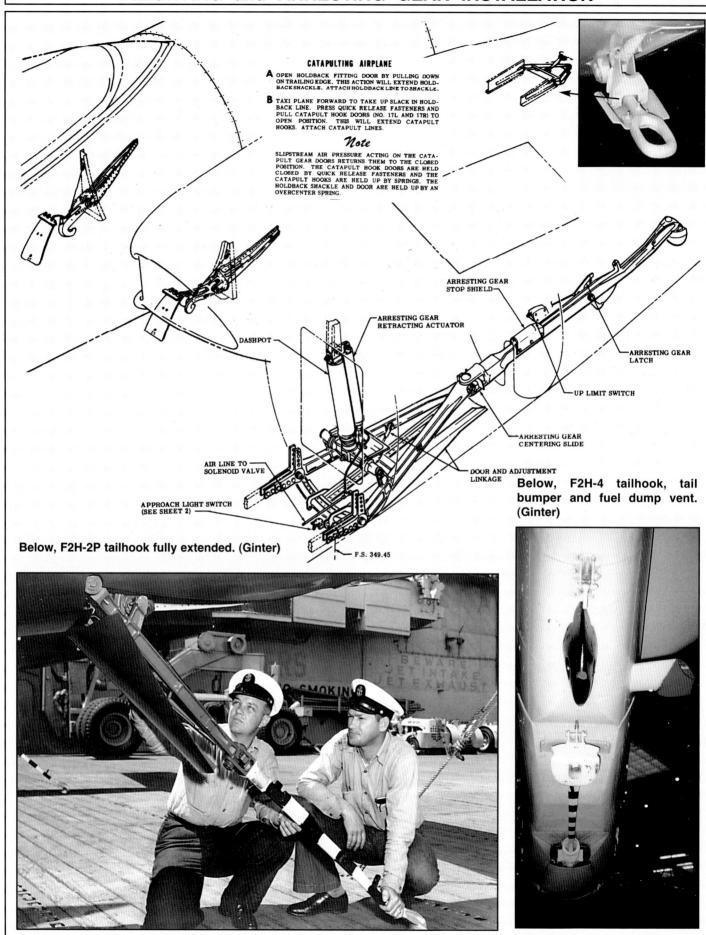

CATAPULTING AIRPLANE

A OPEN HOLDBACK FITTING DOOR BY PULLING DOWN ON TRAILING EDGE. THIS ACTION WILL EXTEND HOLD-BACK SHACKLE. ATTACH HOLDBACK LINE TO SHACKLE.

B TAXI PLANE FORWARD TO TAKE UP SLACK IN HOLD-BACK LINE. PRESS QUICK RELEASE FASTENERS AND PULL CATAPULT HOOK DOORS (NO. 17L AND 17R) TO OPEN POSITION. THIS WILL EXTEND CATAPULT HOOKS. ATTACH CATAPULT LINES.

Note

SLIPSTREAM AIR PRESSURE ACTING ON THE CATA-PULT GEAR DOORS RETURNS THEM TO THE CLOSED POSITION. THE CATAPULT HOOK DOORS ARE HELD CLOSED BY QUICK RELEASE FASTENERS AND THE CATAPULT HOOKS ARE HELD UP BY SPRINGS. THE HOLDBACK SHACKLE AND DOOR ARE HELD UP BY AN OVERCENTER SPRING.

DASHPOT

ARRESTING GEAR RETRACTING ACTUATOR

ARRESTING GEAR STOP SHIELD

ARRESTING GEAR LATCH

UP LIMIT SWITCH

ARRESTING GEAR CENTERING SLIDE

AIR LINE TO SOLENOID VALVE

DOOR AND ADJUSTMENT LINKAGE

APPROACH LIGHT SWITCH (SEE SHEET 2)

F.S. 349.45

Below, F2H-2P tailhook fully extended. (Ginter)

Below, F2H-4 tailhook, tail bumper and fuel dump vent. (Ginter)

22

The F2H-3 powerplant consisted of two Model J34-WE-34 Westinghouse turbo-jet engines of 3,150 lbs thrust in the wing center section, one on either side of the fuselage. The F2H-4 used the 3,600 lbs thrust J34-WE-38 engine.

The engine was 120 inches long, 27 inches in diameter, with a frontal area of 5.16 square feet. Dry weight was 1,255 pounds. The compressor was an eleven-stage axial-flow type with a 3.65:1 compression ratio. The combustion chamber was constructed of stainless steel.

Note

ALL PARTS IDENTIFIED AND SHADED MUST BE REMOVED WHEN CHANGING AN ENGINE AS THESE PARTS ARE NOT IN-CLUDED WITH REPLACEMENT ENGINES RECEIVED FROM STOCK. ENGINE BUILT-UP FOR LEFT INSTALLATION SHOWN. RIGHT ENGINE INSTALLATION IS SIMILAR EXCEPT FOR ROUT-ING OF FUEL AND OIL LINES AND REVERSING THE POSITION OF OTHER PARTS.

RIGHT SIDE OF ENGINE

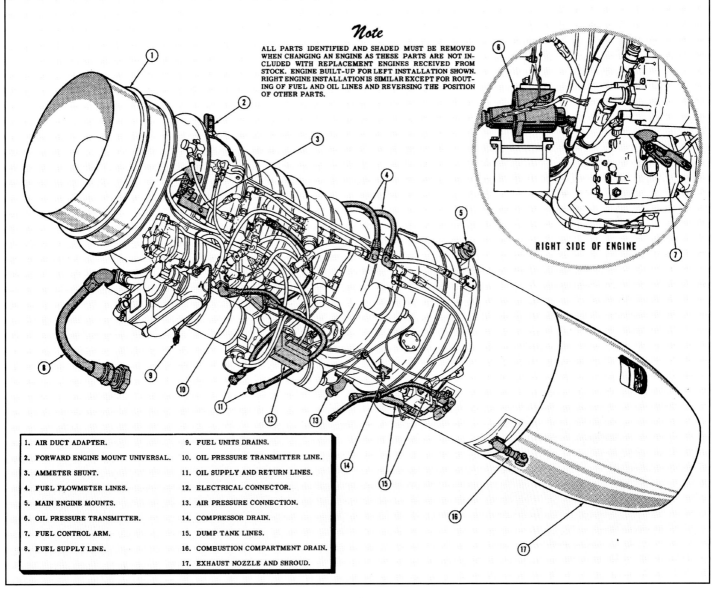

1. AIR DUCT ADAPTER.	9. FUEL UNITS DRAINS.
2. FORWARD ENGINE MOUNT UNIVERSAL.	10. OIL PRESSURE TRANSMITTER LINE.
3. AMMETER SHUNT.	11. OIL SUPPLY AND RETURN LINES.
4. FUEL FLOWMETER LINES.	12. ELECTRICAL CONNECTOR.
5. MAIN ENGINE MOUNTS.	13. AIR PRESSURE CONNECTION.
6. OIL PRESSURE TRANSMITTER.	14. COMPRESSOR DRAIN.
7. FUEL CONTROL ARM.	15. DUMP TANK LINES.
8. FUEL SUPPLY LINE.	16. COMBUSTION COMPARTMENT DRAIN.
	17. EXHAUST NOZZLE AND SHROUD.

F2H-3/4 NOSE GEAR

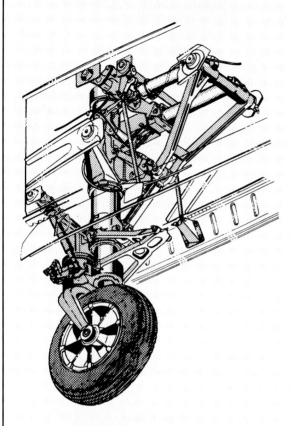

MAIN GEAR STRUT DOOR and FLIPPER DOOR

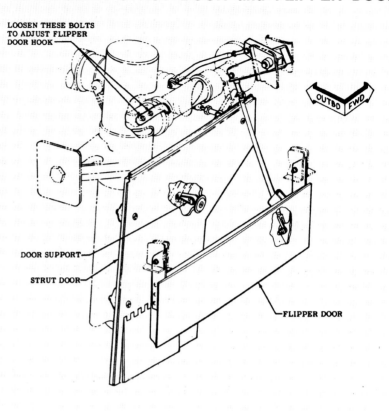

LOOSEN THESE BOLTS TO ADJUST FLIPPER DOOR HOOK

OUTBD FWD

DOOR SUPPORT

STRUT DOOR

FLIPPER DOOR

F2H-3/4 MAIN GEAR

MAIN GEAR WING DOOR

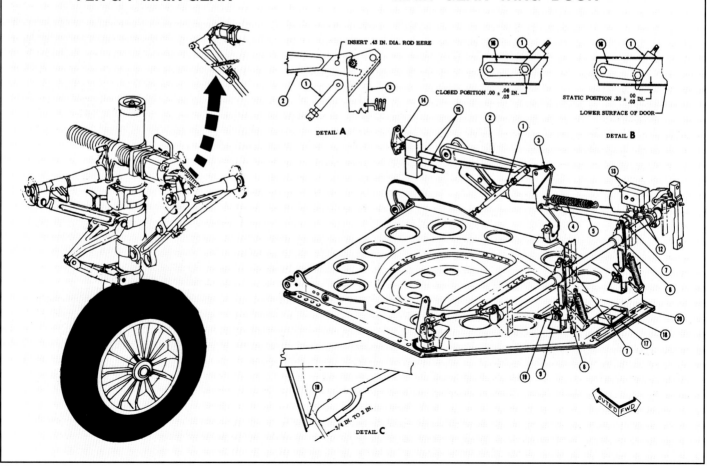

INSERT .43 IN. DIA. ROD HERE

DETAIL A

CLOSED POSITION .00 ± .06/.03 IN.

STATIC POSITION .20 ± .00/.03 IN.

LOWER SURFACE OF DOOR

DETAIL B

3/4 IN. TO 2 IN.

DETAIL C

OUTB'D FWD

Disconnect Points

1. BOLT CONNECTING FLAPPER DOOR ACTUATING ROD TO ARM ON STRUT TRUNNION.
2. PIVOT BOLT ATTACHING STRUT TRUNNION TO STRUCTURE.
3. SAFETY SWITCH WIRING AT SWITCH AND CLIPS ON STRUT TRUNNION.
4. DOWN LIMIT SWITCH WIRING AT SWITCH.
5. ELECTRICAL DISCONNECT PLUG AT ACTUATOR.
6. BOLT ATTACHING ACTUATOR TO SIDE BRACE.
7. PIVOT BOLT ATTACHING SIDE BRACE TO STRUCTURE.
8. DOWN POSITION INDICATOR LIMIT SWITCH WIRING AT SWITCH AND CLIPS ON SIDE BRACE.
9. BOLT ATTACHING LOWER END OF SIDE BRACE TO STRUT.
10. PIN CONNECTING TOGGLE SPRING TO BRACKET ON STRUT TRUNNION.
11. BOLTS ATTACHING ACTUATOR RETRACTING ARMS TO STRUT TRUNNION.
12. BOLT CONNECTING EMERGENCY RELEASE CABLE TO ACTUATOR ARM.
13. BRAKE HYDRAULIC LINE AT STRUT TRUNNION.

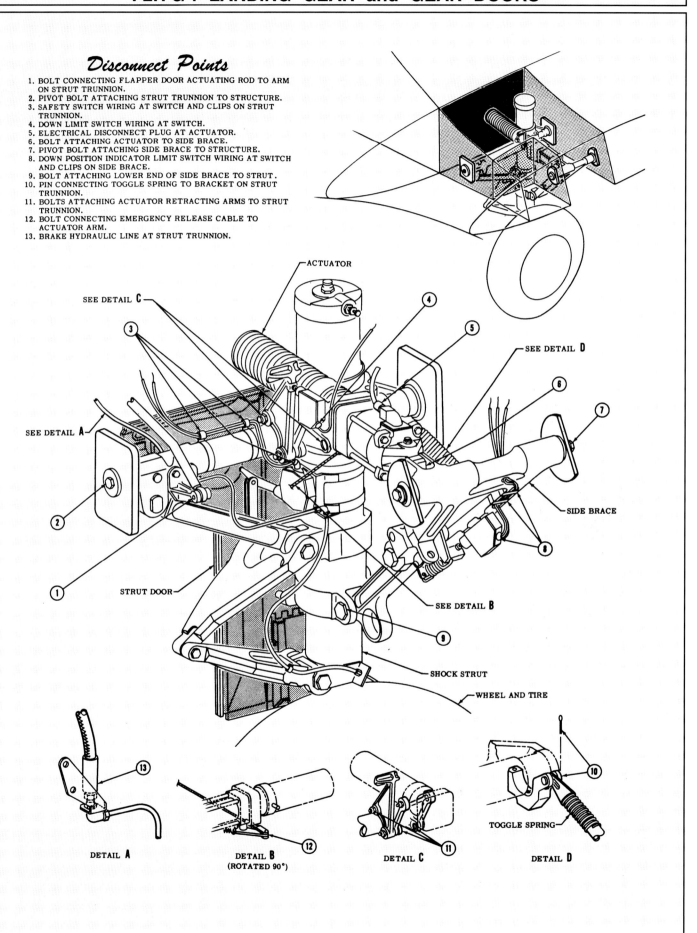

ACTUATOR

SEE DETAIL C

SEE DETAIL A

SEE DETAIL D

SEE DETAIL B

SIDE BRACE

STRUT DOOR

SHOCK STRUT

WHEEL AND TIRE

DETAIL A

DETAIL B
(ROTATED 90°)

DETAIL C

DETAIL D

TOGGLE SPRING

The speed brakes were installed in the outer wing panels forward of the outboard flap. The operation of the speed brake assembly was similar to a parallel bar linkage. The upper and lower perforated plates had two arms at each end which pivoted about a shaft during extension and retraction of the brakes. A electric actuator drove a torque tube system operating the screw jack at each speed brake assembly. Retraction of the screw jacks caused the speed brake assembly to extend from the upper and lower surfaces of the wings.

The four split-type flaps operated down through 60°. Since the flaps were controlled electrically, position selectivity was infinite.

At right, upper wing speed brakes in the extended position. Brakes and outer wing flaps were red inside as was center section flaps. (Ginter) Below, center wing section

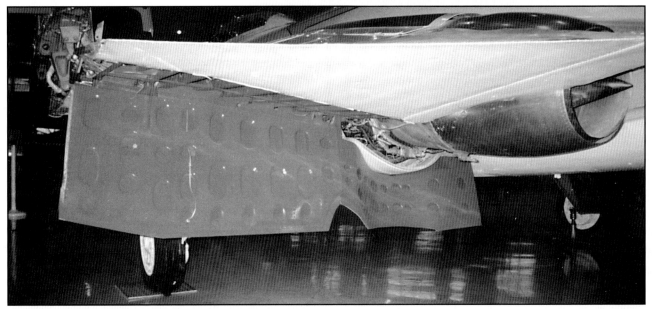

McDONNELL F2H-3/4 WING TIP TANK TIP ASSEMBLY

1. LEFT WING
2. FORWARD BALL SOCKETS
3. FORWARD HOOK
4. AFT HOOK
5. AFT BALL SOCKETS
6. FORWARD TANK BALLS
7. AIR DISCONNECT FITTING
8. FUEL DISCONNECT FITTING
9. TIP TANK
10. ELECTRICAL CONNECTOR
11. AFT TANK BALLS
12. AFT TANK PIN
13. ELECTRICAL CONNECTOR
14. FUEL LINE FITTING
15. AIR LINE FITTING
16. TANK VENT AIRSCOOP

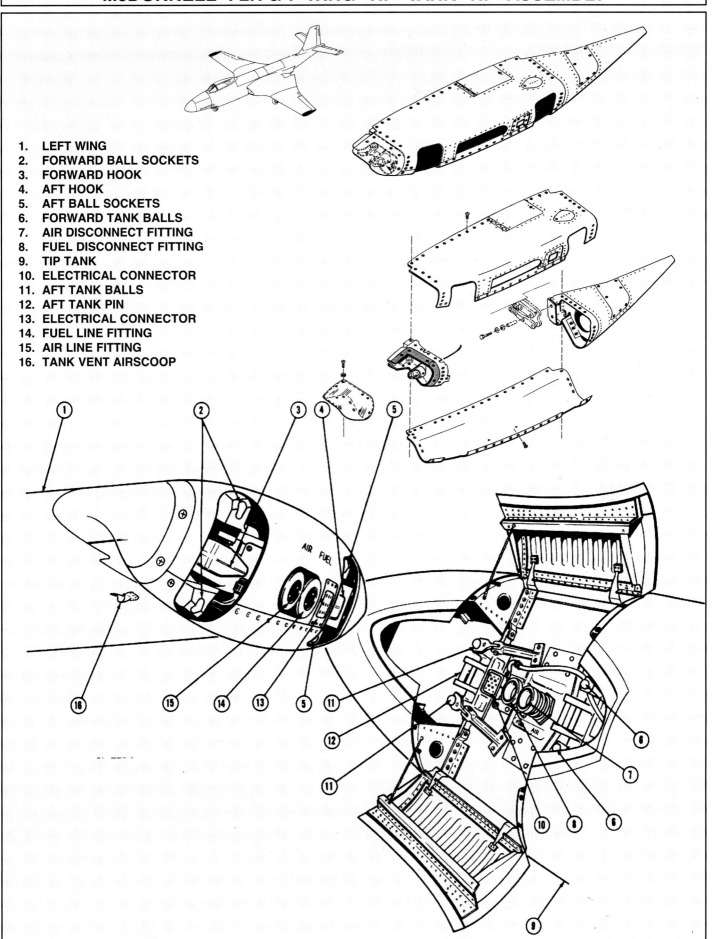

The major components of the wing fold mechanism were a wing fold actuator, and linkage which consisted of a yoke and a link. The electrically operated linear action actuator was used to fold each wing in an upward and inboard direction. The two actuators were installed in the center wing panel structure just aft of the rear spar on both sides of the airplane. The inboard end of each actuator was attached through a universal joint to a support assembly at F.S. 252.2, B.L. 55.4, and W.L. 17.3. The outboard end of the actuator was connected to the outer panel through a yoke and guide link mechanism.

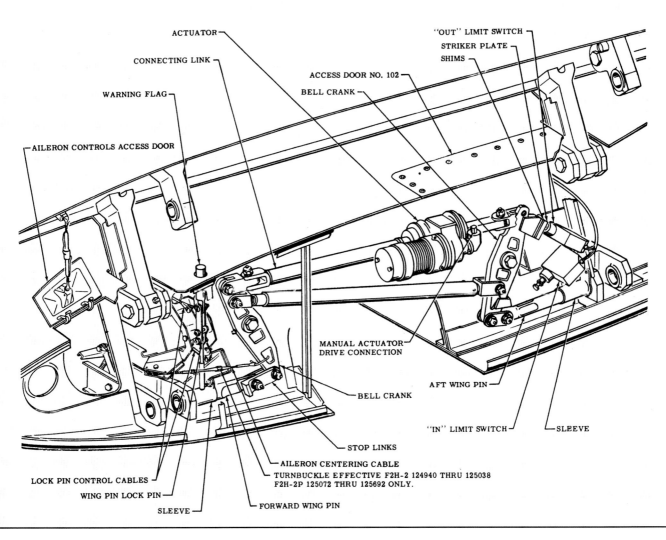

ACTUATOR

CONNECTING LINK

WARNING FLAG

AILERON CONTROLS ACCESS DOOR

"OUT" LIMIT SWITCH

STRIKER PLATE

SHIMS

ACCESS DOOR NO. 102

BELL CRANK

MANUAL ACTUATOR DRIVE CONNECTION

BELL CRANK

AFT WING PIN

"IN" LIMIT SWITCH

SLEEVE

STOP LINKS

AILERON CENTERING CABLE
TURNBUCKLE EFFECTIVE F2H-2 124940 THRU 125038
F2H-2P 125072 THRU 125692 ONLY.

LOCK PIN CONTROL CABLES

WING PIN LOCK PIN

SLEEVE

FORWARD WING PIN

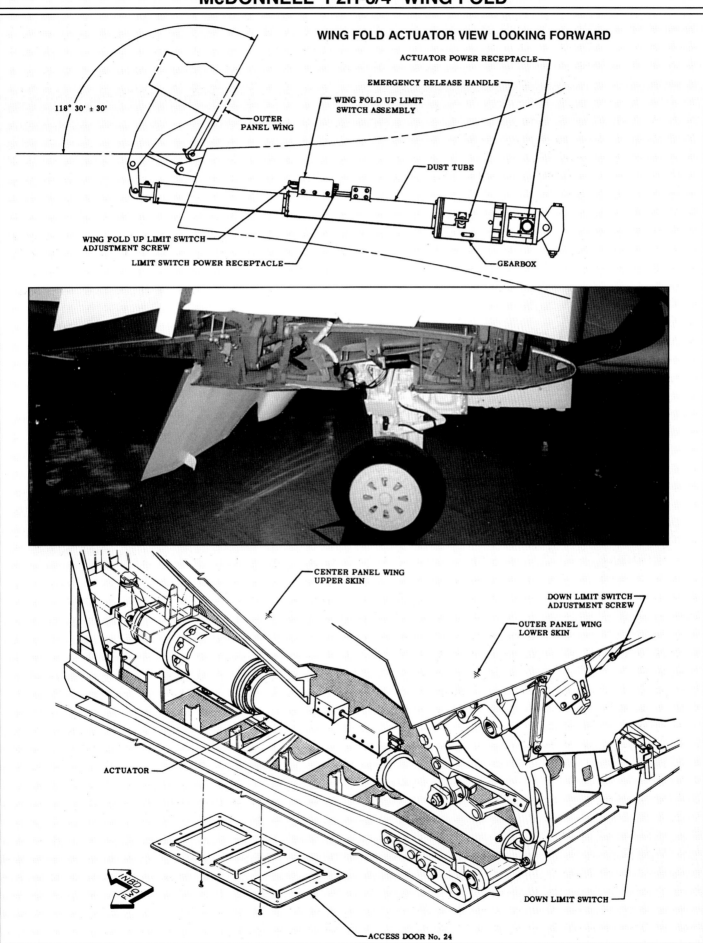

WING FOLD ACTUATOR VIEW LOOKING FORWARD

ACTUATOR POWER RECEPTACLE

EMERGENCY RELEASE HANDLE

WING FOLD UP LIMIT
SWITCH ASSEMBLY

118° 30' ± 30'

OUTER
PANEL WING

DUST TUBE

WING FOLD UP LIMIT SWITCH
ADJUSTMENT SCREW

LIMIT SWITCH POWER RECEPTACLE

GEARBOX

CENTER PANEL WING
UPPER SKIN

DOWN LIMIT SWITCH
ADJUSTMENT SCREW

OUTER PANEL WING
LOWER SKIN

ACTUATOR

DOWN LIMIT SWITCH

INBD
FWD

ACCESS DOOR No. 24

ARRESTING GEAR TRIALS NAS LAKEHURST

NATIONAL ADVISORY COMMITTEE FOR AERONAUTICS, NACA

The National Advisory Committee for Aeronautics (NACA) operated only one Big Banjo, F2H-3 BuNo 126300, from 31 July 1954 through 29 September 1959. It was assigned to NACA Langley and given NACA number 210. However its duties are unknown. It was removed from Navy lists in January 1958.

Above, the 1st production F2H-3 BuNo 126291 conducts simulated carrier landing tests on 5 March 1954 at NAS Lakehurst. (NMNA) Below, NACA 210 was F2H-3 BuNo 125300 seen here in faded gloss sea blue scheme with yellow NACA tail stripe. (via Burger)

NAVAL AIR MISSILE TEST CENTER, NAMTC, POINT MUGU, CA

The Naval Air Missile Test Center (NAMTC) operated one F2H-3 Banshee starting in February 1955. The aircraft was redesignated F2H-3M in June 1955 after modifications made it uneconomical for it to be returned to its previous condition. A second F2H-3M was added in July 1956 and the two aircraft operated at NAMTC until February 1957 when one was transferred out. The remaining F2H-3M continued to operate until May 1958.

FLEET AIR SERVICE SQUADRONS, FASRONS

From 1 January 1947 through 1960, shore based FASRONS were responsible for the majority of maintenance on Navy aircraft. After 1960, the parent squadron was responsible for all maintenance short of overhaul.

Although fifteen different Fleet Air Service Squadrons operated the F2H-3/4 Banshee, no photographic evidence was found. Below is a list of all FASRONS that operated them.

FASRON Two NAS Quonset Pt., RI; FASRON Three NAS Norfolk, VA; FASRON Four NAS North Island, CA; FASRON Five NAS Oceana, VA; FASRON Six NAS Jacksonville, FL; FASRON Seven NAS North Island CA; FASRON Eight NAS Alameda, CA; FASRON Nine NAS Cecil Field, FL; FASRON Ten NAS Moffett Field, CA; FASRON Eleven NAF Atsugi, Japan; FASRON Twelve NAS Miramar CA; FASRON One Zero Four NAF Port Lyauty, Italy; FASRON One-Seventeen NAS Barbers Point, TH; FASRON One-Nineteen NAF Sangley Point, PI; and FASRON One-Twenty MCAF Iwakuni, Japan.

NAVAL AIR TEST CENTER (NATC), PATUXENT RIVER, MARYLAND

The Naval Air Test Center (NATC) is located at NAS Patuxent River, MD, and is responsible for determining an aircraft's suitability for use with the fleet. In the 1950s, NATC project pilots and engineers were divided among five test divisions: Flight Test (FT) concerned itself with airplane and engine performance, stability and control, and carrier suitability; Service Test (ST) evaluated operational and tactical suitability, emphasizing maintenance; Electron- ics Test (ET) reported on all avionics equipment; Tactical Test (TT) to evaluate tactical flying suitability; and Armament Test (AT) conducted an evaluation of the airplane as a weapons platform.

Additionally, the NATC supplied an evaluation team to the contractor's plant for a Navy Preliminary Evaluation (NPE), a formal series of tests with the prototype models prior to the production aircraft's arrival at

Above, F2H-3 BuNo 126352 at Bolling Field in 1953 while assigned to the Tactical Test Division of NATC. TT-10 was painted on the forward fuselage. (NMNA) Below, F2H-3 BuNo 126323 at Patuxent River on 26 November 1952. Aircraft was natural metal with blue tip tanks. (National Archives) Bottom, carrier suitability trials of F2H-3 BuNo 126323. (Fred Roos collection)

NAVAL AIR TEST CENTER
NATC
PATUXENT RIVER, MD

Above, F2H-3 BuNo 126323 landing aboard the USS Antietam (CVA-36) on 14 January 1953. (National Archives) At left, F2H-3 BuNo 126323 during Carrier Suitability Tests aboard the USS Coral Sea (CVA-43) on 29 October 1953. (NMNA) Below, another F2H-3, BuNo 126294, traps aboard the USS Antietam (CVA-36) on 14 January 1953. TT-1 stood for Tactical Test Division aircraft number one. (National Archives)

PAX River. The Board of Inspection and Survey (BIS), while independent of the NATC, also conducted fleet suitability evaluations using the test center's aircraft. Finally, Service Test Division aircraft and personnel were involved in the Fleet Introductory Program (FIP), which trained the first squadron pilots and ground crews scheduled to operate the new aircraft in the fleet.

Above, Armament Test Division (AT-19) F2H-4 BuNo 126352. (NMNA) Below, F2H-3 BuNo 126293 on the USS Midway (CVA-41) on 14 August 1952. (National Archives)

Two photos of F2H-3 BuNo 126292 during carrier trials aboard the USS Coral Sea (CVA-43) on 28 October 1953. (National Archives)

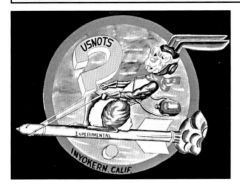

The Naval Air Facility, China Lake, CA, provided support to the Naval Ordnance Test Station (NOTS) for research, development, test and evaluation of guided missiles, aircraft weapons delivery systems, aircraft rockets and rocket launchers, aviation fire control systems, and underwater ordnance.

The F2H-3 Banshee was heavily involved in the development and testing of the 30.5 inch Bombardment Aircraft Rocket (BOAR) delivery vehicle fitted with a TX-7 (Mk. 7) nuclear warhead. It was 183 inches long and weighed between 1,645 and 1,700 lbs. with pit. When installed on the F2H, ground clearance was established by folding the bottom tail fin, one of three on the Mk. 7. Ten different versions of the Mk. 7 were produced and the Mod 0 version (seen at right) featured a rubberized de-icing nose cone boot to minimize radar propagation attenuation for the radar transmit/receive antennas that were located there.

The BOAR was retained in the Navy's inventory from 1956 through 1963 by adapting the A4D Skyhawk to be it's prmary delivery system.

At right top-to-bottom: three views of a BOAR/TX-7 shape being loaded on F2H-3 BuNo 126424 on 18 March 1954. Note cutout in the flaps and extended main gear struts to gain the height required to carry the weapon. The BOAR was painted white, da-glo, and black. (USN via Gary Verver)

Above, two separate special weapons launch tests from F2H-3 BuNo 126404 of the TX-7 shape. Tip tanks were white and the shape was white and da-glo red-orange. (USN via Gary Verver) Below, F2H-3 BuNo 126424 on the ground with another TX-7 shape. Tail writing reads NAF NOTS Inyokern. (USN via Gary Verver)

UTILITY SQUADRON TWO, VU-2

Above right, the last Atlantic Fleet Banshee, an F2H-4 JE/32 belonging to VU-2, prepares to taxi out for its retirement flight in October 1959. LTJG E.C. Quandt was at the controls. The squadron's four F2H-4s were replaced by North American FJ-3 Furies. (USN) At right, F2H-4 127647 JE/33 at NAF Litchfield Park, AZ, on 21 March 1960. (William Swisher)

Below, VX-3 family photo with three Banshees, a F2H-3, F2H-2, and a F2H-2N, in company with a squadron Panther and Skyraider. (National Archives)

NAS Atlantic City-based VX-3 was established on 20 November 1948 by the merger of VF-1L and VA-1L from CVLG-1. CDR W. H. Kingsley, former CO of CVLG-1, took command of the new squadron. Late in 1949, VX-3 received its first jets, the FH-1 Phantom and F2H-1 Banshee. In June 1951, CAPT Gaylor (CO) and LT Reit made the first two jet landings aboard a CVL (USS Wright) in squadron F2H-2s. Based on this initial test, it seemed feasible that jets could operate from CVLs. To further test these conclusions, VX-3 repeated the test with a variety of jet types.

Because of the squadron's mission, VX-3 flew every type of fighter and attack aircraft in the Navy's inventory. The squadron's main mission was threefold: to evaluate new and already existing naval aircraft, airborne equipment and methods; recommend methods for the most effective tactical employment of aircraft and equipment; and to recommend training procedures and countermeasures for these aircraft and methods.

In the spring of 1954, VX-3 operated a F2H-3 aboard the Lake Champlain as a camera ship for the Cinerama movie, "The Thrill of Your Life," which was filmed around carrier operations of VF-103's Cougars. The aircraft's radome was replaced with a wide-angle camera with a sweep of 148° horizontally and 55° vertically and some protective sheet metal.

In March 1954, a three-week cruise aboard the USS Bennington from Mayport, FL, was conducted with VX-3 aboard. During the cruise, the unit carried out carrier qualifications in the F9F, F2H-3/4 and the AD-

Above, VX-3 F3H-3 BuNo 126356 was modified as the Warner Brothers Cinerama camera ship for the Cinerama movie, "The Thrill of Your Life". It is seen here over CVA-39 in January 1954 in company with VC-62 F2H-2P. (National Archives) Below, BuNo 126356 traps aboard the USS Lake Champlain. (Fred Roos collection)

5/6. Similar operations were conducted with F9F-6/7, F2H-3/4, FJ-3 and F7U-3 aircraft aboard the USS Lake Champlain in June 1955. In July 1955, the squadron tested the new British Mirror Landing System aboard the USS Bennington. The test was carried out using F7U-3/3P, F2H-3/4, FJ-3, F9F-8 and AD-5N aircraft. A total of 611 day and night carrier landings were amassed in a four-day period.

Above, another view of the VX-3 camera ship. (USN) Below, VX-3 F2H-3, F2H-2, F2H-2P, AD-2, and TV-2. (USN) Bottom, VX-3 F2H-4 BuNo 127671 refuels from an AJ-2 Savage tanker assigned to VC-7. (Fred Roos collection)

COMPOSITE SQUADRON THREE, VC-3 "BLUE NEMESIS"

VC-3 was established on 2 May 1949, from Detachment One, Fleet All-Weather Training Unit, Pacific (FAWTUPAC). The squadron transferred from NAS North Island to NAS Moffett Field, CA, in October 1949. At Moffett, the unit flew F6F-5Ns, TBM-3E/3Ns, an AD-2Q, and an SNB-5.

VC-3 was tasked with the mission of providing attack (including special weapons) and night fighter detachments to the Pacific Fleet. To fulfill its mission, the unit received F4U-5Ns and F8F-1Ns. On 30 November 1950, the F3D-2 arrived followed by the F2H-2B and the F2H-3 Banshees.

In August 1954, VC-3 took on the added mission of training new squadron personnel in the Navy's new high performance aircraft. Six officers and 36 enlisted men would participate in the Fleet Indoctrination Program (FIP) at NATC. Upon completion of the 600 hour flight test program, the team would return to Moffett to train a core unit of squadron pilots, usually the CO or XO, ops officer and maintenance officer, who in turn would train the rest of the squadron. In 1954, the FJ-3, F7U, and F9F-6 were received to train transitioning Pacific Fleet squadrons.

July 1953 saw the squadron's first Big Banjo deployment conducted by Det Charlie aboard the USS Kearsarge as part of CVG-11. Next was Det Able aboard the USS Yorktown (CVA-10). Another Det sailed on the USS Essex (CVA-9) from 1 December 1953 through 1954. The small detachment was com-

---

Below, VC-3 family photo with an F3D-2, F2H-2 and F2H-3 BuNo 126302 on 15 December 1952. (National Archives)

Above, NAS Moffett Field, CA, in 1953 with VC-3 aircraft NP/66 and NP/68. (Wayne Russel) Below, VC-3 F2H-3 during carrier qualifications aboard the USS Oriskany (CVA-34) in February 1953. (Jim Berry via Tailhook)

prised of OIC LCDR H.W. Sturdevant and two pilots, LTs E.L. March and W.H. Robinson. Det M deployed their F2H-3s aboard the USS Hornet (CVA-12) during its world cruise from 11 May through 12 December 1954. Det G deployed its F2H-3s from 10 August 1955 through 15 March 1956 aboard the USS Hancock (CVA-19).

OIC LCDR E.W. Holloway with LTs R.I. Kasten, A.J. Weil, E.H. Schorz, R.W. Ambrose, J. Carlin and LTJGs R.N. Orr and R.E. Tobias took

At left, VC-3 F2H-3 on the forward elevator of CVA-34 in February 1953. (Jim Berry via Tailhook) Below, F2H-3 undergoing maintenance at NAS Moffett Field, CA, in 1953. (Jim Berry via Tailhook)

Above, Det Charlie pilots on CVA-33 on 16 February 1953. Left-to-right; unknown, LCDR Gale Burkey, CDR "Tex" Guinn, LCDR Moran, unknown, and LT Brownlee. (Jim Berry via Tailhook) Below, two VC-3 Det Charlie F2H-3s operating over the Western Pacific from CVA-33 in 1953. (Jim Berry via Tailhook)

Above, VC-3 F2H-3 BuNo 127527 carrying a nuclear shape refuels from a VC-6 AJ-2 Savage. (Fred Roos collection) Below, VC-3 Det G F2H-3 BuNo 127518 aboard the USS Hancock (CVA-19) in late 1955. (USN) Bottom, VC-3 F2H-3 BuNo 127511 with red and white barber pole refueling probe. LT R.P. Smith was painted below the canopy rail. The tail stripe was blue with white stars. (Balogh via Menard)

a Det aboard the USS Kearsarge (CVA-33) for 1954-1955 cruise. In 1955, CDR C. Fernandez CO took a Det aboard the USS Wasp (CVA-18). The pilots deployed were Tesch, Murphy, Brown, Franklin, Moore, Hills, Young and Pylant.

From January through June 1956 Detachment Juliet with OIC LCDR D.R. Klingler deployed as part of ATG-3 aboard the USS Shangri-La (CVA-38). Aircraft deployed were BuNos 125340, 126340, 126408, and 127514.

In April 1956, the F4D-1 Skyray arrived at VC-3 and on 1 July 1956 the squadron was redesignated VF(AW)-3. Three other new aircraft

Below right, VC-3 F2H-3 after crashing into the island in 1954. (USN)

At left, CDR W.F. West OIC VC-3 Det Easy USS Oriskany (CVA-34). (USN) Below, Det Easy F2H-3 folds wings after landing on the Oriskany during the 1953-54 cruise. (USN)

Above, VC-3 Det Mike pilots were assigned to USS Hornet (CVA-12) as part of CAG-9 in 1954. The OIC was LT J.W. Jenkins. Note the Det Mike insignia applied to the aircraft's forward fuselage. (USN)

Above, VC-3 F2H-3s assigned to CVA-19 refuel from an AJ-2 in October 1955. (National Archives) At left, two F2H-3 Banshees from CVA-19 in October 1955. (National Archives) Below, VC-3 F2H-3 aboard the USS Princeton in 1953. (Russel via Warren Thompson)

were operated by VF(AW)-3 prior to its disestablishment on 2 May 1958. These were the F3H Demon, F8U Crusader and the A4D Skyhawk.

At right top, VC-3 F2H-3 from the USS Wasp prepairing to refuel from a USAF 421st Refueling Squadron KB-29 over Japan in February 1955. (USN) Middle, VC-3 F2H-3 traps aboard Hancock in July 1954. (USN) Bottom, F2H-3 loaded with eight 250lb bombs launches from CVA-19 in July 1954. (USN)

Above, F2H-3 BuNo 127511 at the San Francisco Air Show on 27 August 1954. (William T. Larkins) Below, VC-3 F2H-3 NP/59 on the USS Coral Sea's port elevator. (McDonnell)

F2H-3's

#127511, VC-3. OVERALL NATURAL METAL WITH BLACK LETTERING.

BLUE WITH WHITE STARS

LT R F SMITH

BLACK

BLACK

NP

NAVY

BLACK

106

RED WITH WHITE STRIPES

#126302, VC-3. OVERALL GLOSSY SEA BLUE WITH WHITE LETTERING.
NATURAL METAL LEADING EDGES. CANOPY TRIANGLE RED OUTLINE AND
LETTERING. NOTE EARLY TAIL. DEC. 1952.

NP

BLACK

72

NAVY
VC3

NATURAL METAL

WHITE

F2H-4 #127590, VC-4, SEPT. 1953. NOTE EARLY TAIL AND NO
TIP TANK PROVISION. OVERALL NATURAL METAL WITH BLACK LETTERING
AND WING-WALK.

DARK GREY

BLACK

NA

48

NAVY

#126467, VC-3, JAN. 1955. OVERALL NATURAL METAL WITH BLACK MARKINGS.

NP

NAVY
VC3

BLACK

6

BLACK

#126356, VX-3, JAN. 1954. OVERALL NATURAL METAL WITH BLACK LETTERING.
NO DATA ON NOSE MODIFICATION. NOTE EARLY TAIL GROUP.

XC

NAVY

BLACK

57

Steve Ginter 1980

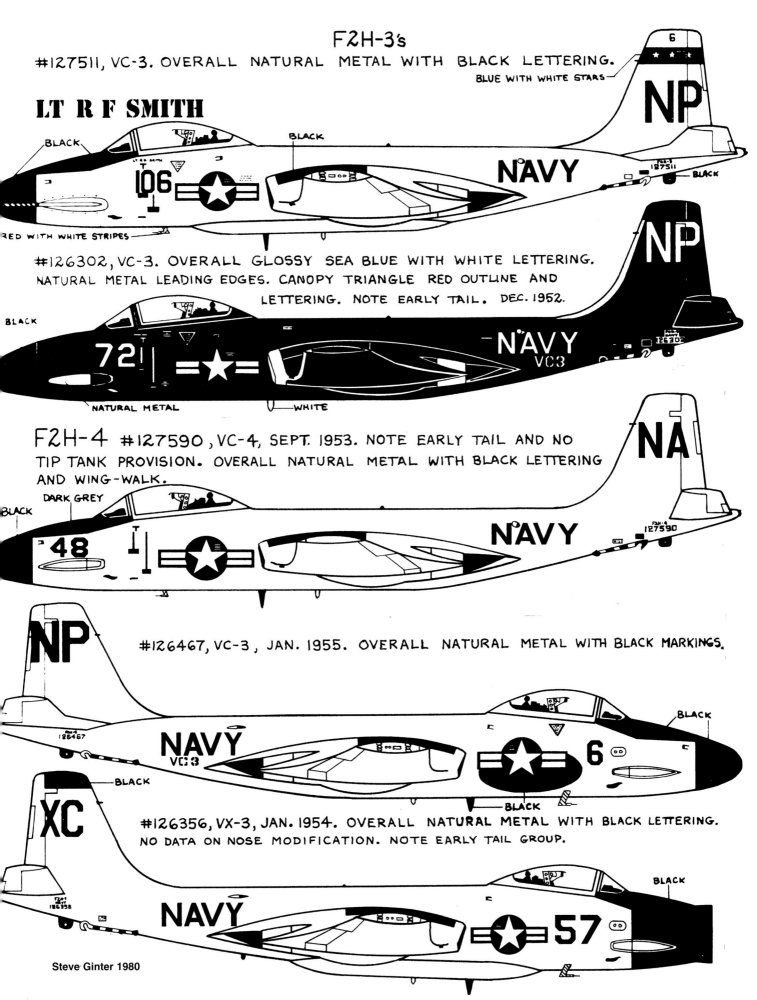

COMPOSITE SQUADRON FOUR, VC-4 "NIGHTCAPPERS"

VC-4 was established at NAS Atlantic City, NJ, on 28 September 1948 as the AIRLANT nightfighter squadron which would supply detachments to deployed carriers. In this role the unit's primary aircraft were F4U-5N/NL Corsairs, F2H-2N/-3/-4 Banshees, and F3D-2 SkyKnights. A small number of non-nightfighters were also used. These included F2H-2/2Bs, F9F-5s and F6F-6s.

The squadron's F2H-2Ns were first operated at night from a carrier in October 1950. They were aboard the USS F.D. Roosevelt (CVB-42), for its seven-week shakedown cruise off the coast of Guantanamo Bay, Cuba. At the time of the deployment, the VC-4 training syllabus consisted of 80-hours in daylight and 55-hours in night operations before a pilot was released for fleet nightfighter service. Both day and night phases were divided into familiarization, navigation, tactics, instruments, gunnery,

Above, VC-4 all-blue F2H-4 BuNo 127588 in May 1955. (Fred Roos collection) Below, VC-4 F2H-3 over Atlantic City on 9 September 1953. (National Archives)

bombing, and field carrier landing practice.

Squadron F2H-2B Banshees (nuc capable) and F4U-5N Corsairs deployed to the Med as part of CVG-17 aboard the USS Coral Sea (CVB-42) from 9 September 1950 through 1 February 1951. Det 6 took its Banshees and Corsairs back aboard the Coral Sea as part of CVG-4 from 19 April through 12 October 1952. Det 5 F2H-2B Banshees and F3D-2 SkyKnights deployed to the Mediterranean aboard the USS Midway (CVA-41) from 1 December

Above and below, VC-4 F2H-3s over Atlantic City on 9 September 1953. (National Archives)

1952 through 19 May 1953. Det 44 also deployed with F2H-2Bs and F3D-2s to Korea aboard the USS

Lake Champlain (CVA-39) from 26 April through 4 December 1953 as part of CVG-4. Det 6 deployed its 3 F2H-3s and 2 F2H-2Bs aboard the USS Coral Sea (CVA-43) from 26 April 1953 through 21 October 1953. Det 35 deployed 4 F2H-4s aboard the USS Midway (CVA-41) for its world

cruise from 27 December 1954 through 14 July 1955. Det 34 deployed aboard the USS Lake Champlain (CVA-39) in 1954-55 and from 9 October 1955 through 30 April 1956.

The squadron was redesignated

Above and below, four VC-4 F2H-3s in flight near Mount Fuji in December 1953. A small white "NA" tail code appears on the upper fin tip. (USN via Swisher)

VF(AW)-4 on 2 July 1956 and the unit was disestablished in July 1959.

Above, VC-4 F2H-4 C/603 in flight in December 1955. (McDonnell) Below, LT Tim Wooldridge in a VC-4 Big Banjo assigned to the USS Lake Champlain (CVA-39) tanking from a VC-5 AJ-2 Savage on 28 January 1955. (National Archives) Bottom, VC-4 Det 34 F2H-4 being towed on the deck of CVA-39 in late 1954. Fin tip and tip tanks were red. Note red metal intake screens. (USN)

Above, three VC-4 F2H-4's Det 34 have their nose numbers repeated below the Air Group's "C" tail code. The squadron's "NA" tail code appears above the tail stripe. Tip tanks had stylized arrows applied to them. (National Archives) Below, VC-4 BuNos 127668 (T/601), 127594 (T/602), and 127588 (T/603). Fin tip was red. 127588 had gloss sea blue tip-tanks. (LCDR Keith D. Boyer via Dave Lucabaugh)

VC-4

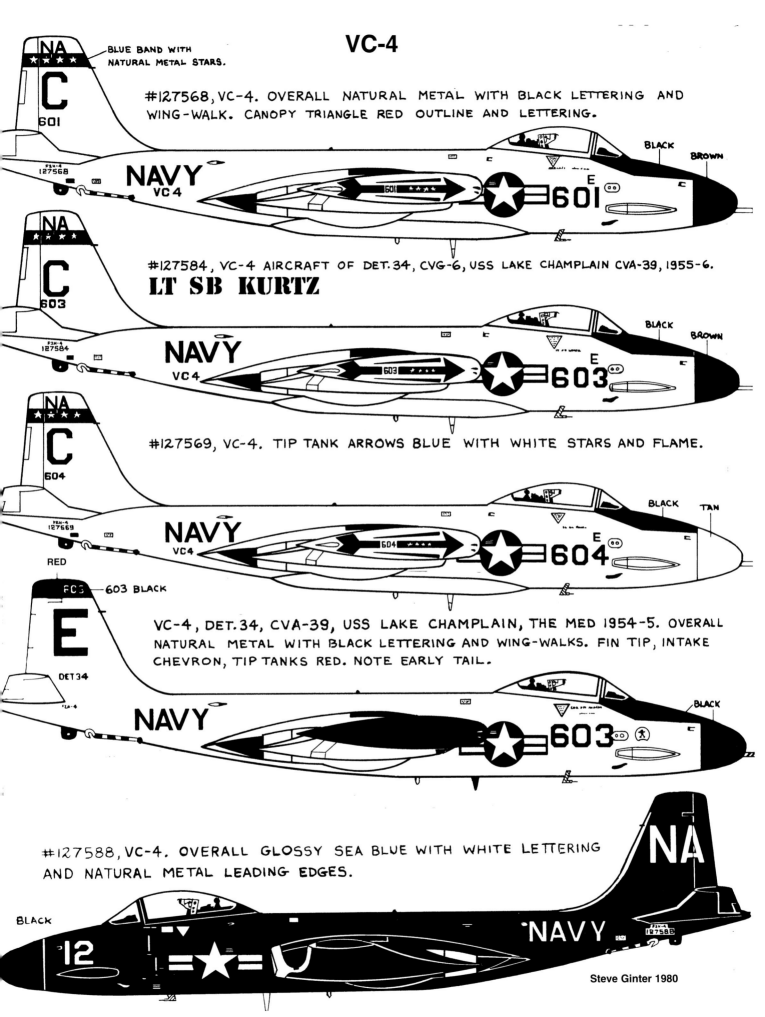

BLUE BAND WITH NATURAL METAL STARS.

#127568, VC-4. OVERALL NATURAL METAL WITH BLACK LETTERING AND WING-WALK. CANOPY TRIANGLE RED OUTLINE AND LETTERING.

BLACK

BROWN

#127584, VC-4 AIRCRAFT OF DET. 34, CVG-6, USS LAKE CHAMPLAIN CVA-39, 1955-6.

LT SB KURTZ

BLACK

BROWN

#127569, VC-4. TIP TANK ARROWS BLUE WITH WHITE STARS AND FLAME.

BLACK

TAN

RED

FO3 — 603 BLACK

DET34

VC-4, DET. 34, CVA-39, USS LAKE CHAMPLAIN, THE MED 1954-5. OVERALL NATURAL METAL WITH BLACK LETTERING AND WING-WALKS. FIN TIP, INTAKE CHEVRON, TIP TANKS RED. NOTE EARLY TAIL.

BLACK

#127588, VC-4. OVERALL GLOSSY SEA BLUE WITH WHITE LETTERING AND NATURAL METAL LEADING EDGES.

BLACK

Steve Ginter 1980

55

Above and below, two VC-4 Big Banjos during carrier operations aboard the USS Intrepid (CVA-11) in January 1955. Some early Banjos were finished without tip tank wing tips as seen here. (National Archives)

ALL WEATHER FIGHTER SQUADRON FOUR, VF(AW)-4 "NIGHTCAPPERS"

The Nightcappers of VC-4 were redesignated VF(AW)-4 on 2 July 1956. Like VC-4, a number of four and five-plane Dets deployed aboard carriers; Det P deployed five aircraft aboard the USS Antietam (CV-36) in 1956. In June 1958 there were 11 F2H-3s and 23 F2H-4s. In June 1959 24 F2H-4s were on-hand. The unit was disestablished in July 1959. After retirement most squadron aircraft were transferred to the reserves at NAS Oakland, CA.

Above, in 1959 a number of the squadron's F2H-4s were enhanced with orange lightning bolts on the tail and fuselage spine as seen here on BuNo 127630. (USN)

F2H-4's

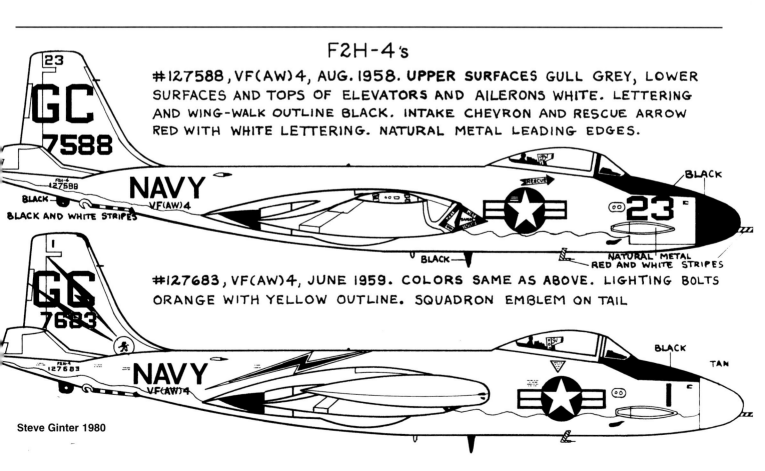

#127588, VF(AW)4, AUG. 1958. UPPER SURFACES GULL GREY, LOWER SURFACES AND TOPS OF ELEVATORS AND AILERONS WHITE. LETTERING AND WING-WALK OUTLINE BLACK. INTAKE CHEVRON AND RESCUE ARROW RED WITH WHITE LETTERING. NATURAL METAL LEADING EDGES.

#127683, VF(AW)4, JUNE 1959. COLORS SAME AS ABOVE. LIGHTING BOLTS ORANGE WITH YELLOW OUTLINE. SQUADRON EMBLEM ON TAIL

Steve Ginter 1980

Above, VF(AW)-4 F2H-4 BuNo 127580 at NAS Quonset Point, RI, on 27 January 1959. (NAH) Below, VF(AW)-4 F2H-4 BuNo 127588 at NAS Patuxent River, MD, on 24 August 1958. (Fred Roos collection) Bottom, VF(AW)-4 F2H-4 BuNo 127683 at Quonset Point in June 1959. Lightning bolts were orange outlined in yellow. (Gordon Blake via Ron Picciani)

AIR DEVELOPMENT SQUADRON FIVE, VX-5 "VAMPIRES"

Originally known as Air Development Squadron Five, VX-5 was established on 18 June 1951 at NAS Moffett Field, CA, with fifteen officers, 100 enlisted men and nine AD Skyraiders Its initial mission was to develop and evaluate aircraft tactics and procedures for the delivery of airborne special weapons. The squadron's mission evolved to include independent operational test and evaluation of all air-dropped munitions destined for use in the attack role by the Fleet and Marine Corps; development of initial tactics to employ new weapon systems; and incorporation of electronic warfare advances into the self-defense capability of attack aircraft.

In July 1956, the squadron moved to NAF China Lake, CA, thereby enabling the unit to take better

Below, gloss sea blue VX-5 aircraft in the blimp hangar at Moffett on 15 October 1952. Visible are two F2H-3s, four F2H-2/2Bs, six ADs, and one JRB. (National Archives)

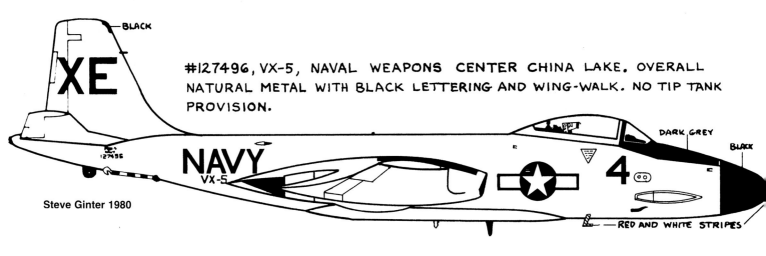

BLACK

XE

#127496, VX-5, NAVAL WEAPONS CENTER CHINA LAKE. OVERALL NATURAL METAL WITH BLACK LETTERING AND WING-WALK. NO TIP TANK PROVISION.

DARK GREY

BLACK

NAVY
VX-5

4

Steve Ginter 1980

RED AND WHITE STRIPES

Below, VX-5 F2H-3 BuNo 127496 on 7 December 1954 flying a low-level, low-ceiling delivery approach. Below right, VX-5 pilots pose in front of 127496 in 1954. Bottom, in flight with da-glo shape. (usn via Gary Verver)

advantage of the vastly improved ranges and technical facilities at China Lake.

In 1969, the unit's designation was changed to Air Test and

Evaluation Squadron Five. In June 1993, the base closings and realignments resulted in VX-4 being combined with VX-5 to create today's Operations and Test Evaluation Squadron Nine (VX-9) Vampires.

AIRBORNE EARLY WARNING SQUADRON ELEVEN, VAW-11 "EARLY ELEVEN"

VC-11 Det J was redesignated VAW-11 in July 1956. At the time it became one of the largest squadrons in the Navy. In January 1959, the unit had 49 AD-5Ws, 23 AD-5Qs, 12 F2H-4s and 1 SNB. VAW-11 was to provide F2H-4 Sidewinder armed Dets to the ASW carriers. One such Det, Det P, deployed aboard the USS Hornet (CVS-12) for a Westpac cruise from 3 April through 10 October 1959. On 16 April, ENS L.L. Marshall was killed in a deck crash. This was the last fleet deployment of the Big Banjo and VAW-11 was the last fleet squadron to retire the F2Hs.

Below, four VAW-11 F2H-4s BuNos 127612 (RR/771), 126456 (RR/776), 127611 (RR/778), and 127607 (RR/777) with Sidewinders in July 1959. (NMNA)

FIGHTER SQUADRON ELEVEN, VF-11 "RED RIPPERS"

VF-11 was established on 1 February 1927 as VF-5 at Hampton Roads, VA. The squadron started flying Curtiss F6C-3s then transitioned to: Boeing F3B-1s, F4B-1s, Grumman FF-1s, F3F-1s and were flying F4F-3s when WWII broke out. VF-5 became VB-5S (7-1-27), VF-5B (1-1-28), VB-1B (7-1-28), VF-5B (7-1-30), VF-5S (7-1-32), VF-5B (4-1-33), VF-4 (7-1-37), VF-41 (3-15-41), and then VF-4 (8-4-43). After the war, with F6F Hellcats, they became VF-1A on 15 November 1946. On 2 August 1948, the squadron was redesignated VF-11 and acquired the F8F Bearcat. In May 1950, they transitioned to the

F2H-1 Banshee for a short period of time before receiving F2H-2s. In April 1953, F2H-4s started replacing the -2 Banshee, but in June were replaced with Douglas F3D-2 SkyKnights. These were in turn replaced rather quickly starting in December with F2H-4 all-weather Banshees. On 28 February 1954, squadron complement was 12 F2H-4s and 1 F3D-2. As part of CVG-10, VF-11 deployed their F2H-4s to the Med aboard the USS Coral Sea (CVA-43) from 7 July through 20 December 1954.

The F2H-4s were temporarily replaced with F2H-2s in late 1955, with 9 being on strength on 30 November. By December 1955 the squadron was flying the F2H-4 once again. In May 1956, fourteen pilots won individual "E"s for outstanding performance in loft bombing.

While still with CVG-10 the unit deployed its F2H-4s again aboard the Coral Sea from 13 August 1956 through 11 February 1957, taking part in the Suez Crises in October 1956. 1958 saw the squadron aboard the USS Essex (CVA-9) while under the command of CDR William B. Allen, where they took part in the Lebonon

Crises in July 1958, and the Quemoy/Matsu islands dispute off the China coast in September 1958. During the cruise, when LT Charles Z. (Bobo) Webb made his 100th landing on Essex, it meant all 16 VF-11 pilots were Essex Centurions. The ship had originally departed Mayport for this cruise and returned there via the Cape of Good Hope on 17 November 1958.

The first VF-11 was disestablished on 15 February 1959 and on 16 February, VF-43 was redesignated VF-11.

Above right, VF-11 F2H-4s aboard the USS Coral Sea (CVA-43) in November 1954. (National Archives) At right, VF-11 gull grey and white F2H-4s P/1XX and blue VF-62 F2H-3s P/2XX on 8 July 1954 as part of CVG-10 aboard the USS Coral Sea (CVA-43) in the Med. (Naval History via Tailhook) Below, two VF-11 F2H-4s in flight near Jacksonville, FL, in February 1954 while assigned to Air Group 10 with BuNo 127654 (P/103) in the foreground. Canopy trim, anti-glare panel, fin tip, and lightning bolts were red outlined in white. (NMNA)

Above and below, three VF-11 F2H-4s: one in natural metal finish (P/106), one in gloss sea blue finish (P/103) and one in gull grey and white finish (BuNo 127570, (P/102) on 2 December 1955 at NAS Cecil Field, FL. (Fred Roos collection) At right, three VF-11 Banshees aboard the USS Coral Sea (CVA-43) in 1954. (USN) At left top, VF-11 F2H-4 in 1956 after returning to CVA-43. Aircraft had landed aboard the USS Randolph and was "zapped" by VF-102. Note VF-11 has been changed to VF-102 and Randolph's "X" tail code was applied to the tail as well as rudder and fin tip diamonds. (NMNA) At left, VF-11 F2H-4 on the elevator of CVA-43 in 1954 while a VC-62 F2H-2P photo-plane is prepared for a mission. (NMNA)

VF-11 "RED RIPPERS"

Above, VAH-11 AJ-2 refuels a VF-11 F2H-4 near Jacksonville on 10 January 1958. (NMNA) At left, VF-11 pilots pose in front of a squadron F2H-4 during the 1958 Essex deployment. (USN) Bottom, two VF-11 F2H-4s BuNos 127598 (AP/110) and 127678 (AP/103) over the Med while assigned to the USS Essex (CVA-9) in 1958. (NMNA)

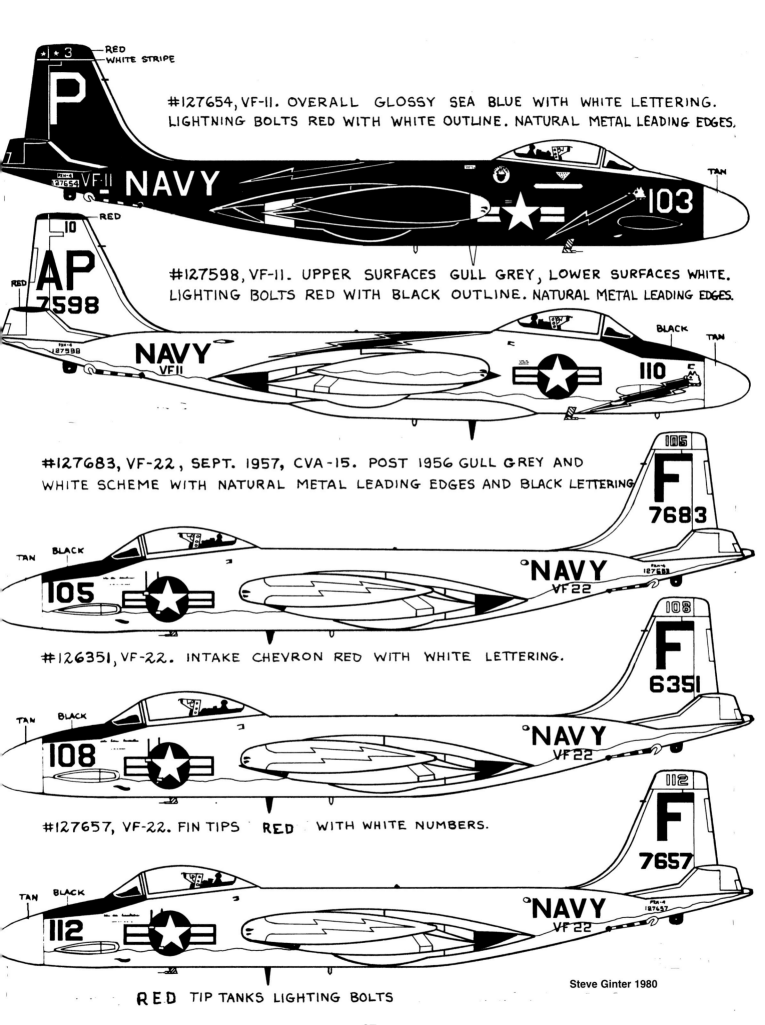

RED
WHITE STRIPE

P

#127654, VF-11. OVERALL GLOSSY SEA BLUE WITH WHITE LETTERING. LIGHTNING BOLTS RED WITH WHITE OUTLINE. NATURAL METAL LEADING EDGES.

VF-11
127654
NAVY
103
TAN

RED

AP
7598

RED

#127598, VF-11. UPPER SURFACES GULL GREY, LOWER SURFACES WHITE. LIGHTING BOLTS RED WITH BLACK OUTLINE. NATURAL METAL LEADING EDGES.

NAVY
VFII
127598
110
BLACK
TAN

#127683, VF-22, SEPT. 1957, CVA-15. POST 1956 GULL GREY AND WHITE SCHEME WITH NATURAL METAL LEADING EDGES AND BLACK LETTERING

F
7683

TAN BLACK
105
NAVY
VF 22
127683

#126351, VF-22. INTAKE CHEVRON RED WITH WHITE LETTERING.

F
6351

TAN BLACK
108
NAVY
VF 22

#127657, VF-22. FIN TIPS RED WITH WHITE NUMBERS.

F
7657

TAN BLACK
112
NAVY
VF 22
127657

RED TIP TANKS LIGHTING BOLTS

Steve Ginter 1980

FIGHTER SQUADRON TWENTY - TWO, VF-22 "CAVALIERS"

VF-22 was established as VBF-74A on 1 May 1945 and was redesignated VBF-74 on 1 August 1945.

After the war, the squadron was redesignated VF-2B on 15 November 1946 and VF-22 on 1 September 1948.

During the Korean War, the squadron operated the F2H-2. The squadron's last deployment with the F2H-2 was aboard the USS Intrepid (CVA-11) in 1955 and 1956. After returning to Jacksonville, VF-22 began transitioning to F2H-4s with 13 on hand on 31 March 1956 along with the squadron's last F2H-2.

VF-22 was honored to take part in the shakedown cruise of the USS Saratoga (CVA-60) as part of CVG-4 from October 1956 through March 1957.

The Big Banjo deployed aboard the USS Randolph (CVA-15) from 1 July 1957 through 24 February 1958. In 1958 while flying a mixed bag of F2H-3 and F2H-4s, VF-22 was disestablished on 6 June 1958.

Below, VF-22 F2H-4s BuNos 126351 (F/108), 127683 (F/105), 127857 (F/112) and 127690 (F/113) on 1 September 1957. (NMNA)

Above, VF-22 F2H-4 BuNo 127690 in flight on 1 September 1957. (USN) Below, VF-22 F2H-4s BuNos 126351 (F/108), 127683 (F/105), 127857 (F/112) and 127690 (F/113) from the USS Randolph (CVA-15) on 1 September 1957. (NMNA)

At top, VF-22 F2H-4 BuNo 126351 taxis on the deck of the USS Saratoga (CVA-60) on 3 September 1956. (NMNA) Above, VF-22 F2H-4 BuNo 127684 at NAS Jacksonvile, FL. (USN) Below, VF-22 F2H-3 BuNo 127657 with "AD" tail code during the launch cycle on the USS Randolph (CVA-15) in 1958. (NMNA) Bottom, VF-22 F2H-4 BuNo 127602 catches a wire on the fly on-board CVA-15 in 1958. (NMNA)

VF-22

At right, VF-22 F2H-4 BuNo 127663 being refueled on the USS Randolph (CVA-15) in October 1957. The pilot's name was written on the fuselage side beneath the windscreen. It was CDR D.E. Douglas; below that on "E" award and the squadron insignia and nose art reading "Big Dan". (via Tailhook) Below, VF-22 F2H-4 AD/103 on Randolph in October 1957. Fin tip was red. (via Tailhook)

FIGHTER SQUADRON TWENTY - THREE, VF-23 "THE FLASHERS"

VF-23 was established on 6 August 1948 at NAS Oceana flying the F4U-5 Corsair. The F9F-2 was received on 4 January 1951 and the squadron made two Korean War deployments.

In March 1953, the squadron transitioned to the F2H-3 Banshee and CDR W.J. Moran took command in July. The squadron boarded the USS Essex (CVA-9) and deployed to the Far East from December 1953 through July 1954. When the Viet Minh attacked the French at Dien Bien Phu in March 1954, the Essex was ordered to operate off the coast of Vietnam.

March 1956 found VF-23 aboard the USS Yorktown (CVA-10) as part of ATG-4. During the cruise the squadron visited Sasebo, Kobe, Beppu, Subic Bay, Manila, Hong Kong and Okinawa. On 4 July 1956, the squadron conducted a flyover of Manila during the joint American-Philippine Independence Day celebration observed by Vice President Richard M. Nixon and Philippine president Ramon Magsaysay. During the cruise every pilot of VF-23, commanded by CDR W.H. Neal III, qualified for day and night operations.

On 11 December 1956 the F4D-1 Skyray started replacing the squadron's F2H-3s. In November 1958 the

Below, all-blue VF-23 F3H-3 BuNo 126435 on CVA-33 as part of ATG-2 in 1953. Aircraft had a red stripe on the fin above the "M" tail code. (NMNA)

Skyrays were traded in for F3H-2 Demons and on 23 February 1959 VF-23 was redesignated VF-151. In 1964 the F-4B Phantom was received. VF-151 received F/A-18 Hornets and was redesignated VFA-151 on 1 June 1986.

VF-23 F2H-3 makes a hard landing aboard the USS Essex (CVA-9) and collapses its landing gear in 1954. (USN)

Above, two VF-23 Big Banjos in flight. (USN) Below, VF-23 F2H-4 BuNo 127530 while assigned to the USS Yorktown (CVA-10) in June 1956. Outer half of tip tanks were red and white candy stripes as was narrow stripe above the tail code. (USN)

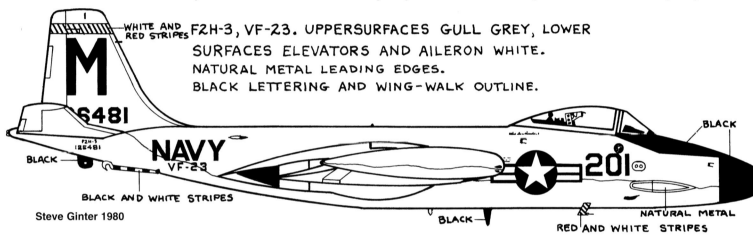

WHITE AND RED STRIPES F2H-3, VF-23. UPPERSURFACES GULL GREY, LOWER SURFACES ELEVATORS AND AILERON WHITE.
NATURAL METAL LEADING EDGES.
BLACK LETTERING AND WING-WALK OUTLINE.

M

6481

F2H-3
126481

NAVY
VF-23

BLACK

BLACK AND WHITE STRIPES

BLACK

201

BLACK

NATURAL METAL

RED AND WHITE STRIPES

Steve Ginter 1980

At top, natural metal VF-23 F2H-3 127530 at NAS Oakland, CA, on 26 September 1954. Wing tips and fin tip stripe were red. (Larry Smalley) Above, VF-23 yellow-tailed F2H-3 BuNo 126481 near San Francisco, CA. (via Rich Dan) Below, three VF-23 F2H-3s escort a VC-61 F2H-2P in July 1956. (USN) Bottom, F2H-3 BuNo 126417 in flight from CVA-10 IN 1956. (National Archives)

VF-23

Above and at right, VF-23 F2H-3s refuel from a Convair R3Y-2 Tradewind in 1956. BuNos 127539 M/107 and 126348 M/108. (USN) Below, flight of seven VF-23 F2H-3s from CVA-10 in July 1956. BuNos 127511 M/209, 126348 M/209, 127543 M/203, 126361 M/205, 126401 M/201, 127509 M/204 and 126417 M/206. (National Archives)

FIGHTER SQUADRON THIRTY - ONE, VF-31 "TOMCATTERS"

Fighter Squadron Thirty-One started out life as VF-1B on 1 July 1935 with F4B-4s. Redesignated VF-6 on 1 July 1937, the squadron flew F3Fs and later F4Fs. On 15 July 1943, VF-6 became VF-3 and transitioned to F6F Hellcats. On 15 November 1946, the squadron became VF-3A and transitioned to the F8F-1 Bearcat. VF-3A became VF-31 on 7 August 1948 and transitioned to the F9F-2 in December 1949.

1953 found the squadron transitioning, first to F2H-2s in February and then F2H-3 Banshees in March. In October 1953, VF-31 reported to Fleet All Weather Training Unit Atlantic (FAWTULANT) at NAS Key West, FL, where it became the first all-weather jet squadron to be trained in day and night radar intercept tactics. Commanded by CDR P.W. Schlegal, the unit was trained for a month by Capt Price's FAWTULANT.

As part of CVG-6 the squadron deployed its F2H-3s aboard the USS Midway (CVA-41) to the Mediterranean from 4 January through 4 August 1954. Upon their return, the squadron reported to the Navy's newest master jet base at NAS Cecil Field, FL.

In April 1955 carrier qualifications were held aboard the USS Coral Sea (CVA-43) and in May the unit trained in all-weather intercept missions at Key West, FL. This was followed by carrier qualifications aboard the USS

Below, four VF-31 F2H-3s over the USS Midway (CVA-41) in February 1954. Although assigned to CVG-6, the squadron wore CVG-3's tail code. (USN)

Above, VF-31 F2H-3 on the elevator of the USS Midway (CVA-41) in March 1954. Most Banshees used on this cruise were not fitted with tip tank wing tips installed. (National Archives) Below, VF-31 F2H-3 on CVA-41 in 1954. Fin tip, wing tips and nose flash were red. (USN)

Lake Champlain (CVA-39) in October. From 4 November 1955 through 2 August 1956, VF-31 deployed aboard the USS Ticonderoga (CVA-14) as part of CVG-3.

In November 1956, the F3H-2N Demon started replacing the F2H-3 "Big Banjos" which, in-turn, were replaced with the McDonnell F-4B Phantom II in 1963. The squadron's long association with the Phantom ended in 1980 when

Above and below, VF-31 F2H-3s from the USS Midway (CVA-41) in flight on 26 January 1954. (National Archives) At right, natural metal F2H-3 on Midway. Note wing codes. (USN)

F2H-3's OF VF-31

104 — RED WITH WHITE 104

K

#126415, CVA-41, USS MIDWAY, JAN. 1954. OVERALL NATURAL METAL WITH BLACK MARKINGS AND WING WALKS. STYLIZED BIRD MOTIF RED WITH THIN BLACK OUTLINE. WING TIP RED.

F2H-3
126415

NAVY ★104

BLACK

RED

106 — RED WITH WHITE 106

K

#126410. OVERALL GLOSSY SEA BLUE, WHITE LETTERING AND BLACK WING-WALKS. STYLIZED RED BIRD WITH WHITE OUTLINE.

F2H-3
126410

NAVY ★106

BLACK

108

K

#126425. COLOR AND MARKINGS AS ABOVE. IN THE MED 1954.

NATURAL METAL

F2H-3
126425

NAVY ★108

109

K

#126464, LATTER TRANSFERRED TO ROYAL CANADIAN NAVY. COLORS SAME AS #104.

F2H-3
NAVY
126464

NAVY ★109

111

K

#126436. MARKINGS AS #106. NATURAL METAL TIP TANK. NOTE SQUADRON EMBLEM AFT OF CANOPY. ALL AIRCRAFT HAVE EARLY TAIL.

BROWN

F2H-3
NAVY
126436

NAVY ★111

VF-31

RED BOARDER, YELLOW CENTER, BLACK BOMB AND CAT WITH WHITE EYES AND FACE.

Steve Ginter 1980

Above, VF-31 line in 1955. (USN) Below, VF-31 F2H-3 with a nuclear shape tanking from a VC-5 AJ-2 on 12 October 1955. (National Archives) Bottom, two more VF-31 F2H-3s tanking from a VC-5 tanker on 12 October 1955. (National Archives)

FIGHTER SQUADRON FORTY - ONE, VF-41 "BLACK ACES"

The Black Aces started out life as VF-75 on 1 June 1945 at NAAS Chincoteaque, VA. They flew the F4U Corsair and moved to NAS Norfolk in 1947. The squadron was redesignated VF-3B in November 1946 and in September 1948 VF-41. They moved to NAS Jacksonville, FL, in January 1949 where the unit was disestablished for a short period in 1950 and then reestablished at NAS Oceana. The F2H-3 was acquired in July 1953.

As part of ATG-181, VF-41 deployed their F2H-3s aboard the USS Hornet (CVA-12) for two short periods from 18 November through December 1953 and from 6 January

Below, VF-41 F2H-3 BuNo 126464 at Lambert Field, OH. Rudder stripes were yellow/orange. (Fred Roos collection) Bottom, VF-41 F2H-3 during the CVA-59 shakedown cruise. (USN)

through 1 March 1954 to the Caribbean. The Black Aces then deployed aboard the USS Randolph (CVA-15) to the Mediterranean from 30 November through 18 June 1955. For an unknown reason the aircraft on this cruise wore CVG-19's "B" tailcode.

Wearing CVG-6's "C" tailcode, the squadron conducted carrier qualifications aboard the USS Ticonderoga (CVA-14) in January 1955 and took part in the ship's shakedown cruise to Guantanamo Bay, Cuba, beginning on 3 February 1955.

While still assigned to ATG-181, VF-41 had the honor of participating in the shakedown cruise of the World's first Super Carrier, the USS Forrestal (CVA-59), from 24 January through 31 March 1956. The short ten week deployment was conducted in and around Guantanamo Bay, Cuba.

From 3 October 1956 through 23

Above, VF-41 F2H-3 being muscled into position on the deck of CVA-59. (via Nick Williams) Below, VF-41 F2H-3 on Forrestal's elevator. Tip tanks were painted in yellow/orange stripes. (USN)

Above, VF-41 F2H-3 BuNo 126465 with a VMF-533 F2H-4 in the background at the Dayton Airport on 2 September 1954 prior to deployment on the USS Randolph (CVA-15). (via Mark Aldrich) Below, VF-41 F2H-3s at NAS Oceana in 1955. (National Archives) Bottom, maintenance being performed on a VF-41 F2H-3 on 2 September 1953. (National Archives)

May 1957, the squadron deployed aboard the USS Bennington (CVA-20) again as part of ATG-181. On 2 May, the squadron took part in the 15th anniversary of the Battle of the Coral Sea.

The Big Banjo was replaced by the F3H Demon in 1958. The Demons gave way to the F-4 Phantom II in February 1962 and the F-14 Tomcat in April 1976.

Above, VF-41 F2H-3 C/313 traps aboard the USS Hornet (CVA-12) in 1953-54. (Fred Roos collection) Below, VF-41 F2H-3s fly past the USS Randolph (CVA-15) in 1955. (NMNA)

"BLACK ACES"

Above, VF-41 F2H-3 at FAWTU NAS Key West on 5 January 1954. Rudder stripes were red and yellow/orange. (NMNA) At left, VF-41 F2H-3 traps aboard the USS Boxer in 1956 and the right main gear failed. (Ginter collection) Below, VF-41 F2H-3 BuNo 126415 after landing on CVA-15 in 1956. Fin tip and rudder stripes were red. (NMNA)

VF-52 was originally established as VBF-5 on 8 May 1945. Flying the F6F Hellcat, VBF-5 was redesignated VF-6A on 15 November 1946. The squadron was redesignated VF-52 on 16 August 1948.

With F9F-2/2B Panthers, the squadron took part in three Korean War cruises starting in July 1950. The Sealancers made a post-war WEST-PAC cruise with Panthers aboard the USS Wasp (CVA-18) from 1 September 1954 through May 1955 as part of ATG-1.

The squadron began transitioning to the F2H-3 Banshee in May 1955. As part of ATG-1 the squadron oper-

Above, F2H-3 BuNo 126367 traps aboard CVA-16 in 1956. (NMNA) Below, VF-52 F2H-3 assigned to ATG-1 aboard the USS Lexington in 1956. (Fred Roos collection)

ated in the Western Pacific from the deck of the USS Lexington (CVA-16) from 28 May through 20 December

1956.

In 1957, while under the command of CDR C.N. Seaver, the twelve Banshees of VF-52 claimed the West Coast record for most hours flown in a single month. It was 1,036 accident free hours.

As part of ATG-1 the squadron carrier-qualified aboard the USS Ticonderoga (CVA-14) in July-August

At top, VF-52 F2H-3 BuNo 126474 at NAS Moffett Field, CA, on 17 May 1958. Note the ATG-1 yellow-outlined shooting star on the fuselage and the yellow flash aft of the intake chevron. (William T. Larkins) Above left, VF-52 F2H-3 BuNo 127538 with Sidewinder pylons under the wing. (USN) At left, VF-52 F2H-3 BuNo 126324 on the catapult on the USS Ticonderoga (CVA-14) in 1958. USN) Below, VF-52 F2H-3 on CVA-14 in 1958 while assigned to ATG-1. (USN)

1958 and deployed from 4 October 1958 through 16 February 1959 on the Ticonderoga. For this cruise CDR Ray A. Volpi was in command. ATG-1 was disestablished after this cruise and the squadron was disestablished on 23 February 1959.

Above, VF-52 F2H-3 on the catapult of CVA-20 in 1958. (USN) At right, VF-52 F2H-3s BuNos 127498 (NA/206) and 126477 during carrier qualifications aboard the refurbished USS Bennington (CVA-20) in March 1958. (via Tailhook) Below, VF-52 F2H-3 BuNo 126374 in 1958. (NMNA)

FIGHTER SQUADRON SIXTY-FOUR, VF-64 "FREELANCERS"

VF-64 was originally established as VF-81 on 1 March 1944 at NAS Atlantic City, NJ, flying F6F Hellcats. With F8F Bearcats, the squadron was redesignated VF-13A on 15 November 1946. On 2 August 1948 they became VF-131. While equipped with F4U Corsairs, the squadron became VF-64 on 1 December 1949. The squadron entered the jet age in December 1952 when they received the F9F-5 Panther.

VF-64 deployed twice with its Panthers aboard the USS Yorktown (CVA-10) in 1953-54 and the USS Essex (CVA-9) in 1954-55.

After their Panther deployments in July 1955, VF-64 received McDonnell F2H-3 Banshees starting in September. The squadron deployed aboard the USS Shangri-La (CVA-38) in November 1956 through 20 May 1957. Carrier

VF-64 F2H-3 aboard CVA-38 in 1956-57. Tail stripes were red and white. (USN)

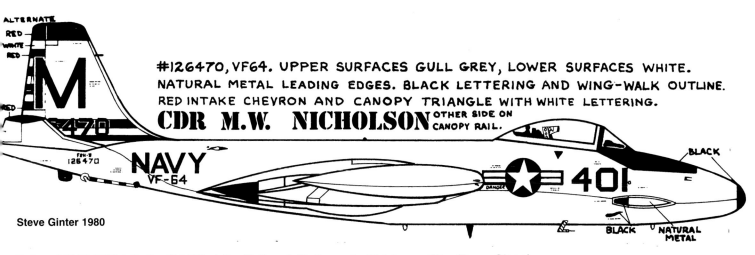

#126470, VF64. UPPER SURFACES GULL GREY, LOWER SURFACES WHITE.
NATURAL METAL LEADING EDGES. BLACK LETTERING AND WING-WALK OUTLINE.
RED INTAKE CHEVRON AND CANOPY TRIANGLE WITH WHITE LETTERING.

CDR M.W. NICHOLSON OTHER SIDE ON CANOPY RAIL.

Steve Ginter 1980

Below, VF-64 F2H-4 BuNo 126470 at the National Air Races in Oklahoma City. (Doug Olson)

qualifications were conducted aboard CVA-38 in August.

The Big Banjos were replaced by the McDonnell F3H-2 Demon starting in December 1957 and the squadron was redesignated VF-21 on 1 July 1959. At the end of 1961 the squadron moved to NAS Miramar, CA. The F-4B Phantom arrived in September 1962. The squadron went on to fly three more versions of the Phantom: the F-4J, F-4S, and F-4N. On 4 November 1983, the last Phantom was transferred out and the squadron began transitioning to the Grumman F-14A Tomcat.

At top, VF-64 F2H-3s BuNos 126470 (M/401) and 127497 (M/402). Flap interior was painted dark red. (A. Krieger via Menard) At left, VF-64 Banshee seen head on. Note the tip tank offset. (A. Krieger via Menard) Below, VF-64 F2H-4 BuNo 126456 (M/407). (A. Krieger via Menard)

FIGHTER SQUADRON SEVENTY-ONE, VF-71
"FICKLE FINGER SQUADRON"/"HELL'S ANGELS"

VGS-18 was established on 15 October 1942 and redesignated VC-18 on 1 March 1943 at NAS Whidbey Island, WA. Initially equipped with twelve FM-1 Wildcats and nine TBM Avengers, thirty-six F6F Hellcats were received in early 1944. During the war, the squadron was credited with 172 kills in the air and 300 planes destroyed on the ground. They were also involved in the sinking of the Japanese battleships Musashi and

Below, VF-71 F2H-3 BuNo 126362 was natural metal with red tail trim. (Don Walsh via NMNA) Bottom, VF-71 F2H-3 traps aboard the USS Bennington (CVA-20) in 1953. (NMNA)

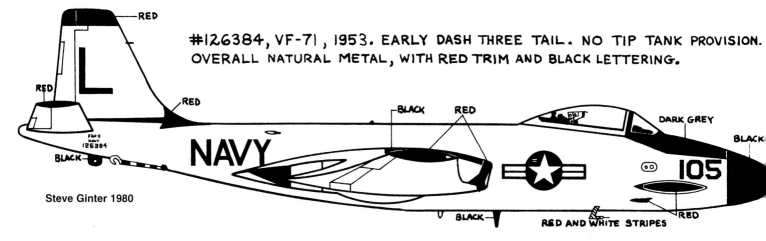

#126384, VF-71, 1953. EARLY DASH THREE TAIL. NO TIP TANK PROVISION. OVERALL NATURAL METAL, WITH RED TRIM AND BLACK LETTERING.

RED
L
RED
RED
RED
BLACK
RED
NAVY
BLACK
RED AND WHITE STRIPES
BLACK
DARK GREY
BLACK
105
RED

Steve Ginter 1980

Yamato. They were known as the "Fickle Finger Squadron" because of the gesturing devil insignia. They were redesignated VF-18 in the summer of 1944 and moved to San Diego, CA, where they equipped with F8F-1 Bearcats. In October 1945, the squadron moved to NAS Quonset Point, R.I., and equipped with F9F-2 Panthers in December 1949. In

October 1951, the squadron was assigned F9F-5s along with VF-72 and VF-73 to conduct service testing on the type. VF-71 and VF-72 reacquired the F9F-2 in the spring of 1952 in time for a Korean War deployment aboard the USS Bon Homme Richard (CV-31) from 21 June through 18 December 1952.

After converting to F2H-3s in June 1953 a post-war Med cruise was conducted aboard the USS Bennington (CVA-20) from 16 September 1953 through 27 May 1954. During the deployment the squadron participated in NATO Exercise Mariner in the North Atlantic. Prior to the cruise, BuNos 126384 (L/105 and 126411 (L/111) collided

Above, VF-71 F2H-3 BuNo 127520 assigned to the USS Intrepid (CVA-11) taxis at NAS Moffett Field, CA, in 1957. Nose stripe and rudder stripe was red with white stars. (via Harry Gann)

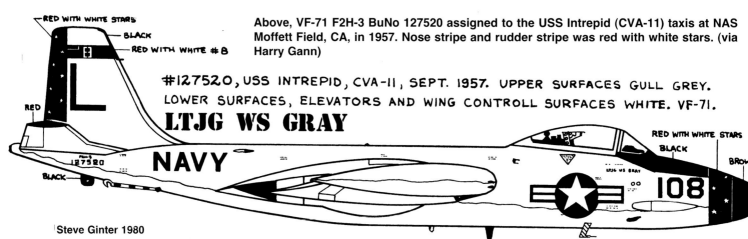

RED WITH WHITE STARS
BLACK
RED WITH WHITE # 8
L
RED
LTJG WS GRAY
NAVY
127520
BLACK
RED WITH WHITE STARS
BLACK
BROW
108

#127520, USS INTREPID, CVA-11, SEPT. 1957. UPPER SURFACES GULL GREY. LOWER SURFACES, ELEVATORS AND WING CONTROL SURFACES WHITE. VF-71.

Steve Ginter 1980

and crashed in Rhode Island on 24 June 1953.

As part of CVG-7, VF-71 deployed aboard the USS Hornet (CVA-12) from 4 May through 10 December 1955. During the cruise the squadron participated in Operation Passage to Freedom, which was the evacuation of citizens from North Vietnam to South Vietnam.

The squadron operated from the USS Intrepid (CVA-11) from April through October 1957. The squadron took part in NATO Operation Strikeback, the largest naval exercise up to that time since WWII, from 7 September until October 1957.

VF-71 conducted a Med cruise aboard the USS Randolph (CVA-15) from 2 September 1958 through 12 March 1959. After returning to CONAS, VF-71 was disestablished on 31 March 1959.

Above, VF-71 F2H-3 AF/112 shares the deck of the USS Intrepid (CVA-11) with ADs and a F4D-1 as a VF-71 Big Banjo comes in for a trap. (via Tommy Thomason) Below, VF-71 F2H-3s aboard the USS Intrepid (CVA-11) during operation Strike Back in September 1957. Tail trim was red with white stars on the rudder. (National Archives)

Below, VF-71 F2H-4s aboard the USS Randolph (CVA-15) in August 1958. (NMNA) At right, VF-71 F2H-4 Big Banjos seen from above during their 1958-59 deployment aboard CVA-15. (NMNA)

FIGHTER SQUADRON EIGHTY - TWO, VF-82 "IRON MEN"

Reserve squadron VF-742 was activated in February 1951 and was initially equipped with F4U-4 Corsairs. In 1952, the F9F-2 Panther replaced the Corsairs. The Iron Men started transitioning to the F9F-5 in September 1952 and completed the transition in November. On 4 February 1953, VF-742 was redesignated VF-82 and in early 1954 the squadron transitioned to the F2H-2B/2N Banshee.

For their 1954-55 cruise, the squadron flew a mixed complement of F2H-2B (special weapons capable) and F2H-2N (night fighter) Banshees. They deployed to the Mediterranean aboard the USS Lake Champlain (CVA-39) as part of CVG-8 from 28 September 1954 through 22 April 1955. After returning, the unit transitioned to the F2H-4 at NAS Oceana, VA, with 14 on-hand on 30 June 1955.

In January 1956, CVG-8 was assigned to the USS Intrepid (CVA-11). That spring they deployed to the Mediterranean, returning on 5 September 1956. After returning to CONUS, the unit transitioned to the McDonnell F3H Demon, which they flew until 15 April 1959 when the squadron was disestablished.

Above, four gloss sea blue VF-82 Banshees surrounded by Skyraiders and Savages on CVA-11 in 1956. (Fred Burton) Below, VF-82 F2H-4 landing on CVA-11 on 20 April 1956. (USN)

Above, VF-82 F2H-4 BuNo 127603. Fin tip and wing tips were red. (Fred Roos collection) Below, VF-82 F2H-4 BuNo 127597 on 21 March 1955. (NMNA) Bottom, VF-82 F2H-4 landing on the USS Intrepid (CVA-11) on 20 April 1956 as part of CVG-8. The nose and tip tanks have red stylized stripes outlined in white with white stars added. (NAH via Tailhook)

FIGHTER SQUADRON NINETY - TWO, VF-92 "SILVER KINGS"

VF-92 was established at NAS Alameda, CA, on 26 March 1952 with F4U-4 Corsairs. The squadron took the name Silver Kings and the motto "Death, Terror, and Vengeance" shortly after standing-up. VF-92 took their Corsairs to war aboard the USS Valley Forge (CV-45) from November 1952 through June 1953. After returning to Alameda, the squadron transitioned to the Grumman F9F-2 Panther.

The Silver Kings made one deployment with the F9F-2 from 12 March through 19 November 1954 aboard the USS Philippine Sea (CVA-47). When the squadron returned from its WESTPAC, they were reassigned to NAS Miramar, CA, where they transitioned to the AD-4 Skyraider. After a Skyraider cruise aboard the USS Shangri-La (CVA-38), the squadron returned to Alameda in June 1956 and acquired the F9F-5 Panther.

In October 1956, the Panthers were replaced with F2H-3 Banshees.

The squadron made three short training cruises aboard the ASW carrier USS Yorktown (CVS-10). Then, as part of CVG-9, VF-92 deployed aboard the USS Ticonderoga (CVA-14) from 16 September 1957 through 25 April 1958

The all-weather association with McDonnell products continued when the F3H-2 Demon was received in September 1958. In June 1962, VF-92 was redesignated VF-54 and received the F-4B Phantom II in July 1963. VF-54 was disestablished in 1975.

Below, VF-92 F2H-3 BuNo 126308 after main gear failure on 24 January 1957. (NMNA)

Above, VF-92 F2H-3 BuNo 126419 aboard the USS Yorktown (CVA-14) in July 1958. Fuselage and tail flash were yellow outlined in black. (Doug Olson via Larkins) At right, The National Museum of Naval Aviation's Big Banjo painted as 126419 above at the NMNA in 1999. (Ginter) Below, 126419 at NAF Litchfield Park on 21 March 1960. (William Swisher) Bottom, VF-92 spine details on F2H-3 BuNo 126416 at NAS Alameda, CA, on 17 May 1958. (William T. Larkins)

FIGHTER SQUADRON ONE ZERO TWO, VF-102 "DIAMOND BACKS"

VF-102 was established on 1 July 1955 at NAS Cecil Field, FL, with F2H-4 Banshees. Assigned to the USS Bennington (CVA-20) from July through November 1955, the unit became part of ATG-202 and took part in the shakedown cruise of the USS Randolph (CVA-15) to the Caribbean from January through March 1956. They then deployed to the Mediterranean aboard Randolph from 14 July 1956 through 19 February 1957.

While in training at NAS Key West, FL, for their upcoming deployment aboard the USS Randolph (CVA-15) VF-102 set new squadron records. In 17 days all 17 pilots qualified with 10 graded as excellent, 3 outstanding and two receiving Navy "E"s. Commanded by CDR Reagan, the unit flew 529 hours during 220 flights. The squadron then returned to NAS Cecil Field, FL, where they concentrated on field carrier landing practice and special weapons delivery.

The squadron transitioned to the Douglas F4D-1 in the spring of 1957 and in August 1961 they began to transition to the F-4B Phantom II.

Above, VF-102 F2H-4 BuNo 127686 Banjo in flight. (NMNA) Below, VF-102 F2H-4 BuNo 127638 traps aboard the USS Randolph (CVA-15) in 1956 as part of ATG-202. Rudder and tail stripe were red with white stars as was the fuselage stripe aft of the radome. (NMNA)

F2H-4's

NOSE AND TAIL MARKINGS RED WITH WHITE DIAMONDS.

#127594, VF-102, 1955-56. UPPER SURFACES GULL GREY. UNDER SURFACES AND ELEVATORS AND WING CONTROL SURFACES WHITE. INTAKE CHEVRON RED WITH WHITE LETTERING. NATURAL METAL LEADING EDGES. LETTERING, WING TIP AND WING-WALK OUTLINE BLACK. CANOPY TRIANGLE OUTLINE AND LETTERING RED.

#127620, VF-102, BOTH AIRCRAFT ON DETACHMENT USS RANDOLPH, CVA-15. NOTE NEW RUDDER MINUS MARKINGS.

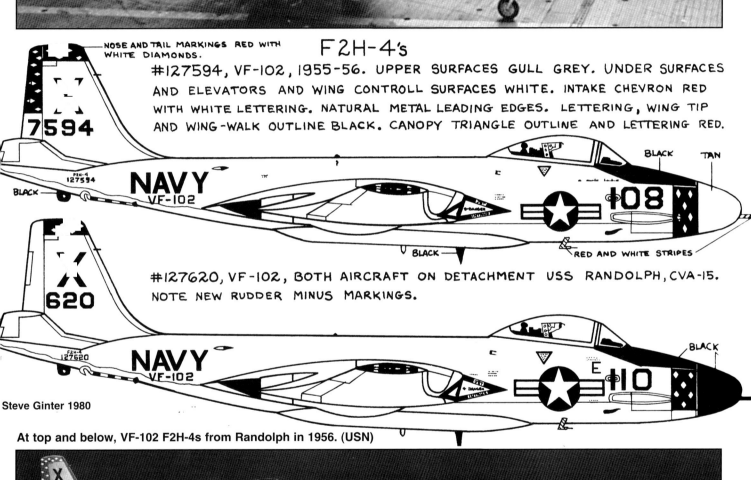

Steve Ginter 1980

At top and below, VF-102 F2H-4s from Randolph in 1956. (USN)

FIGHTER SQUADRON ONE - FOURTEEN, VF-114 "EXECUTIONERS"

VF-114 was originally established as Bombing Squadron Five Bravo (VB-5B) on 2 July 1934 at NAS Norfolk, VA. In July 1937, the squadron was redesignated VB-2. As VB-2, the squadron took the Douglas SBD Dauntless to war. The squadron was disestablished on 1 July 1942 and reestablished as VB-11 on 10 October 1942 with the Curtiss SB2C Helldiver. On 15 November 1945 the squadron was redesignated VA-11A and then VA-114 on 1 July 1948. On 15 February 1950, VA-114 became VF-114. VF-114 received Chance

Vought F4U Corsairs and deployed to Korea aboard the USS Philippine Sea

---

Below, VF-114 F2H-3 BuNo 126430 at NAS Miramar, CA, on 30 October 1955. Anti-glare panel was olive drab and fin tip was orange trimmed in black. (William Swisher) Middle, 126437 at Miramar on 30 October 1955. Pilot's name, LCDR M CUTCHEON, has the VF-114 insignia above it. (via Swisher) Bottom, VF-114 F2H-3 BuNo 126330 in the fog at NAS Los Alamitos, CA, in July 1955. (William Swisher)

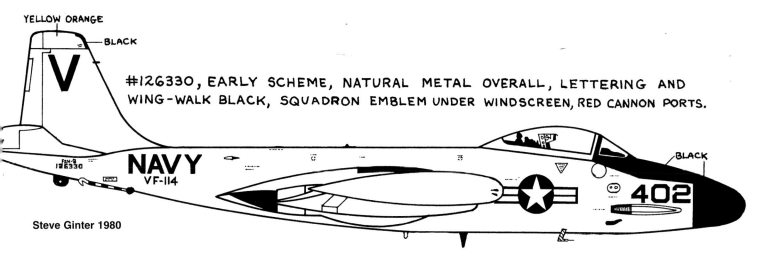

YELLOW ORANGE

BLACK

#126330, EARLY SCHEME, NATURAL METAL OVERALL, LETTERING AND WING-WALK BLACK, SQUADRON EMBLEM UNDER WINDSCREEN, RED CANNON PORTS.

NAVY
VF-114

402

BLACK

Steve Ginter 1980

(CV-47).

Upon return from Korea, VF-114 transitioned to the Grumman F9F-5 Panther in October 1952. The squadron's first Panther deployment was from 1 July 1953 through 18 January 1954 aboard the USS Kearsarge (CVA-33). VF-114 took its F9F-5 Panthers aboard the USS Kearsarge (CVA-33) for a second time from 7 October 1954 through 12 May 1955.

The McDonnell F2H-3 Banshee replaced the Grumman F9F-5 Panthers in June 1955. The squadron deployed its Big Banjos aboard the

Below, gull grey and white VF-114 F2H-3s aboard the USS Essex (CVA-9) in September 1956. (National Archives)

Above, two VF-114 Banjos BuNos 126437 (V/405) and 126419 (V/401) from CVA-9 in 1956. (USN) Below, the USS Essex (CVA-9) approaches Diamond Head in 1956 with a VF-114 Banshee spotted on the catapult. (USN)

USS Kearsarge (CVA-33) as part of CVG-5 from 29 October 1955 through 17 May 1956. Ports-of-call were: Pearl Harbor, Yokosuka, Subic Bay, Manila, Hong Kong, and Iwakuni. The squadron took part in Operations Jack Pratt on 9 December and NAV MAR LEX on 17 February. The cruise was not without tragedy as LTJG William Eberle Hayes was killed on 13 March 1956.

For a second F2H-3 deployment, CDR William C. Smith prepared the squadron for a WestPac cruise aboard the USS Essex (CVA-9) from July 1956 through February 1957.

In March 1957, VF-114 received the McDonnell F3H-2N Demon which was replaced with the McDonnell F4H-1 Phantom in 1961. The squadron went on to fly F-4B and F-4J Phantoms before transitioning to the Grumman F-14A Tomcat in 1976. After operating seventeen years with the Tomcat, the squadron was disestablished on 30 April 1993.

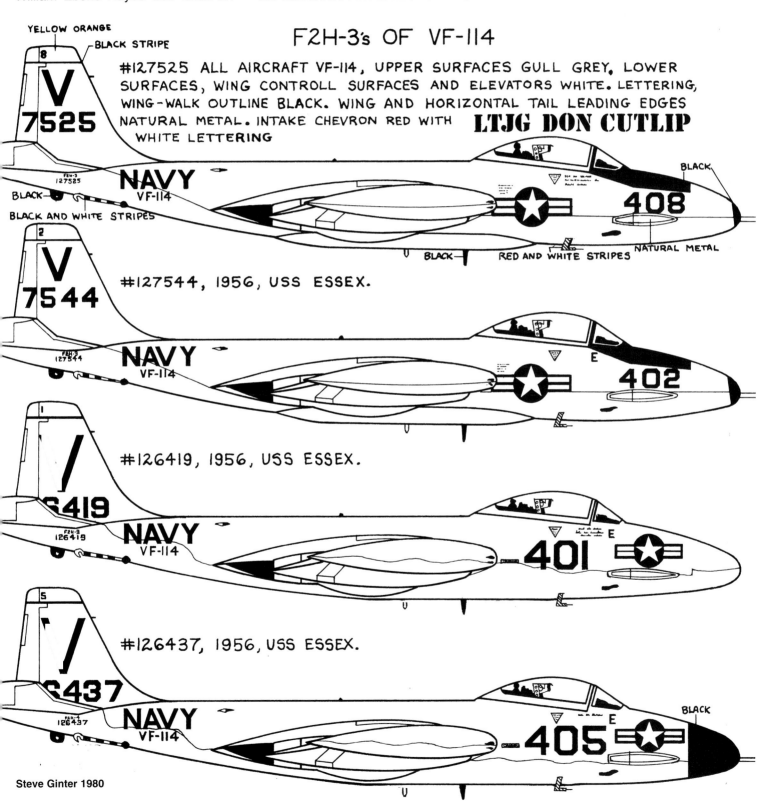

F2H-3's OF VF-114

#127525 ALL AIRCRAFT VF-114, UPPER SURFACES GULL GREY, LOWER SURFACES, WING CONTROLL SURFACES AND ELEVATORS WHITE. LETTERING, WING-WALK OUTLINE BLACK. WING AND HORIZONTAL TAIL LEADING EDGES NATURAL METAL. INTAKE CHEVRON RED WITH WHITE LETTERING

LTJG DON CUTLIP

YELLOW ORANGE
BLACK STRIPE
V 7525
NAVY VF-114
BLACK
BLACK AND WHITE STRIPES
408
BLACK
RED AND WHITE STRIPES
NATURAL METAL

#127544, 1956, USS ESSEX.
V 7544
NAVY VF-114
E 402

#126419, 1956, USS ESSEX.
6419
NAVY VF-114
E 401

#126437, 1956, USS ESSEX.
6437
NAVY VF-114
E 405
BLACK

Steve Ginter 1980

FIGHTER SQUADRON ONE TWENTY - ONE, VF-121 "PACEMAKERS"

Above, VF-121 F2H-4 taxis past two Douglas guppies at North Island on 24 September 1958. (USN)

NAS Los Alamitos reserve squadron VF-781 was established on 1 July 1946 flying F6F-5 Hellcats. The squadron volunteered for active duty 100% at the outbreak of the Korean War in July 1950. LCDR Collin Oveland moved his squadron to NAS North Island where it combined with three other fighter squadrons and one attack squadron to form CVG-102. The squadron started forming-up on the F4U-4 but transitioned instead to F9F-2 Panthers by the end of the year. Due to the overcrowding at

North Island, VF-781 relocated to NAAS Miramar 20 miles away. As a result of the move, VF-781 became the first Navy fighter squadron to be assigned to Miramar after the Marines gave up the base.

On 10 May 1951, CVG-102 reported aboard the USS Bon Homme Richard (CV-31) and left North Island for the war zone. During the second Panther cruise on 4 February 1953, while off the coast of Korea, VF-781 was redesignated VF-121. Once back at Miramar, VF-121 under the command of CDR J. E. Savage, transitioned to the new Grumman F9F-6 Cougar. A Boxer deployment was made and then the

squadron obtained F9F-8 Cougars. The squadron began to transition to the FJ-3M Fury in March 1957 in preparation for its 1957 WestPac deployment aboard the USS Lexington (CVA-16).

In 1958 the F11F-1 was acquired and in April the squadron became the Replacement Air Group (RAG) for both the F11F Tiger and F3H Demon. Training was augmented with two F2H-4s and a number of F3D-2T2s. The two F2H-4s were operated from March through September 1958. In October 1962, they became the F-4 Phantom RAG, a job they performed until their disestablishment in September 1980.

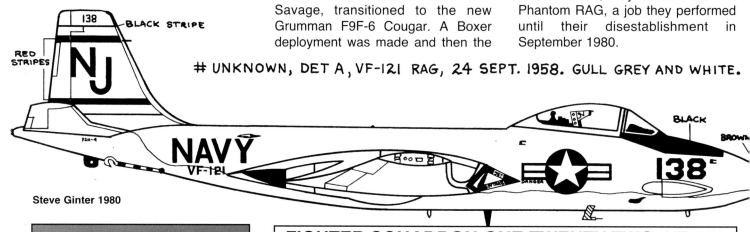

UNKNOWN, DET A, VF-121 RAG, 24 SEPT. 1958. GULL GREY AND WHITE.

Steve Ginter 1980

FIGHTER SQUADRON ONE TWENTY-TWO, VF-122 "BLACK ANGELS"

Reserve squadron VF-783 was called to active duty on 20 July 1950 in response to the Korean War. The squadron deployed to Korea with its F9F-5 Panthers aboard the USS Oriskany (CV-34) from 10 February 1952 through 2 May 1953 as part of CVG-102. While at sea, off the coast of Korea, VF-783 was redesignated VF-122 on 4 February 1953. The squadron utilized the F2H-3 as an

interim aircraft at NAS Miramar, CA, from June through November 1956, with a total of six aircraft being on-hand in September and October. No images of VF-122 F2H-3s were located.

The F3H-2N Demon was received in December 1957 and was flown until the squadron was disestablished on 1 May 1958.

FIGHTER SQUADRON ONE FORTY - ONE, VF-141 "IRON ANGELS"

Reserve squadron VF-721 was called to active duty on 20 July 1950.

CVG-101, with VF-721 attached, deployed to Korea aboard the USS Boxer (CV-21) from 27 March through 30 November 1951.

VF-721 took its F9F-2 Panthers aboard the USS Kearsarge (CV-33) for a second war cruise from 14 September 1952 through 22 April 1953 as part of CVG-101. On 4 February 1953, VF-721 was redesignated VF-141.

Upon returning from the second war cruise, the Iron Angels transitioned to the McDonnell F2H-3 Banshee in March 1953. After workups, the squadron deployed to the Mediterraean aboard the USS Randolph (CVA-15) from February through August 1954 while under command of CDR Frank Standring. After more training at Miramar, the squadron deployed its Banshees one last time aboard the USS Kearsarge (CVA-33) from October 1955 through March 1956 under the command of

---

Below, VF-141 F2H-3 BuNo 126433 had a red fin tip. (NMNA) Bottom, VF-141 F2H-3 BuNo 126434 bolters while trying to trap aboard the USS Randolph (CVA-15) on 21 July 1954 in the Med. (NMNA)

CDR W. Weigold.

The squadron stepped up to the Douglas F4D-1 Skyray in June 1956 and the McDonnell F3H-2 Demon in 1959. In May 1962 the Demons were replaced with the Vought F-8E Crusader. VF-141 was redesignated VF-53 on 15 October 1963. As VF-53, the squadron flew the F-8E and F-8J Crusader. VF-53 was disestablished on 29 January 1971.

Above, VF-141 F2H-3s on CVA-15 in 1954. The natural metal aircraft have olive drab anti-glare panels. Below, CVA-15 anchored off Naples with the USS Midway (CVA-41) on 20 July 1954. (National Archives)

Above, VF-141 F2H-3s BuNos 126441 (A/106) and 127619 (A/101) aboard Randolph in 1954. (Warren Thompson) Wing and fin tips were red. (Warren Thompson) At right, VF-141 F2H-3 BuNo 126474 prepped for launch from the USS Kearsarge (CVA-33) in 1955. (Warren Thompson) Below, four gull grey and white VF-141 Banshees pass Mt. Fuji on 10 February 1956. (NMNA)

FIGHTER SQUADRON ONE FIFTY - TWO, VF-152 "FIGHTING ACES"
ATTACK SQUADRON ONE FIFTY - TWO, VA-152 "FRIENDLIES"

The squadron made two deployments as part of CVG-15 to the Western Pacific. The first was aboard the USS Yorktown (CVA-10) from 1 July 1954 through 28 February 1955. The second was aboard the USS Wasp (CVA-18) from 23 April through 15 October 1956. During the Yorktown cruise the unit flew night surveillance operations in support of the evacuation of Chinese Nationalists from the Tachen Islands.

Reserve Fighter Squadron Seven Hundred Thirteen (VF-713) was called to active duty on 1 February 1951 and received F4U-4s as replacements for their F8Fs. On 4 February 1953, VF-713 was redesignated VF-152 and transitioned to F2H-3s in November 1953.

As part of ATG-4, the squadron deployed aboard the USS Hornet (CVA-12) from 6 January through 2 July 1958. In March, the squadron operated in the South China Sea off of Indonesia due to insurrection and revolts in the region. After returning from this deployment, the squadron was redesignated VA-152 on 1

August 1958.

Below, VF-152 F2H-3 taxiing on the deck of the USS Yorktown (CVA-10) in 1956. Note orange lightning bolts on the tail. (NMNA)

Above, natural metal VF-152 F2H-3 launching from CVA-10 in 1956. (NMNA) Below, VF-152 F2H-3 BuNo 127529 traps aboard USS Wasp (CVA-18) in June 1956. Note unusual placement of the national insignia on the aircraft's nose and special weapons pylon. (NMNA) Bottom, VF-152 F2H-3 taxis forward after trapping on Wasp in 1956. (USN)

113

VF-152 F2H-3s from CVA-10 coded H/202 (blue), H/203, H/204, H/208, & H/210 in flight in 1956. (NMNA)

Above, VF-152 F2H-3 BuNo 127533 at NAS Moffett Field, CA, on 18 May 1957. Fin flash, fin tip, and nose and tip tank arrows were yellow outlined in black. (William T. Larkins)

The squadron's final deployment with the Banshee was aboard the USS Bennington (CVA-20) as part of ATG-4 from 21 August through 12 January 1959. VA-152 operated off Taiwan in September and October after the Communist Chinese began shelling the Chinese Nationals.

The squadron received AD-6 and AD-7 aircraft on 5 February 1959 and 1962 respectively. These were replaced with A-4B/Cs in February 1968 and A-4Es in May 1969. VA-152 was disestablished on 29 January 1971.

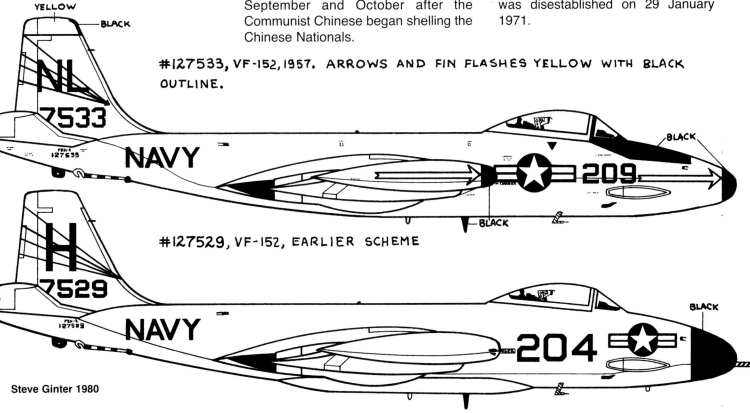

#127533, VF-152, 1957. ARROWS AND FIN FLASHES YELLOW WITH BLACK OUTLINE.

#127529, VF-152, EARLIER SCHEME

Steve Ginter 1980

Below, VA-152 F2H-3s BuNos 126417 (ND/210), 127519 (ND/209), and 127515 (ND/205) in 1958 while assigned to the USS Bennington (CVA-20). (Fred Roos collection)

FIGHTER SQUADRON ONE SEVENTY - ONE, VF-171 "ACES"

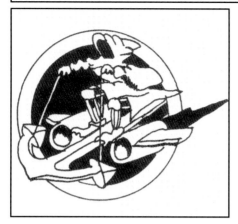

VF-82 was established at NAS Atlantic City, NJ, on 1 April 1944 and was redesignated VF-17A on 15 November 1946. On 11 August 1948, VF-17A was redesignated VF-171. With VF-172 as part of CVG-17, the two squadrons transitioned to the McDonnell FH-1 Phantom. Two short Caribbean deployments were made with the Phantoms prior to receiving the F2H-1 Banshee.

In August 1949, carrier qualifications with the F2H-1 were conducted aboard the USS F.D. Roosevelt (CVB-42). On 3 September 1949, LT "Diz" Laird covered the 432 miles from the deck of the USS Midway to the Cleveland National Air Races with a record average speed of 476 knots. CVG-17 conducted carrier trials with the F2H-1 on the USS Philippine Sea (CV-47) in December 1949.

VF-171 deployed its F2H-2 Banshees exclusively on the navy's three big post-war CVB class carriers Midway, F.D. Roosevelt and Coral Sea. The first was aboard CVB-43 to the Mediterranean from 9 September 1950 through 1 February 1951. This was followed by a short stint to the Caribbean aboard CVB-41 from 22 May through 10 July 1951. Three

more deployments were made, all aboard CVB/CVA-42. These were from 3 September 1951 through 4 February 1952 to the Med, 23 June through 4 August 1952 to the Caribbean, and 26 August through 19 December 1952 to the North Atlantic.

In January 1953, the squadron transitioned to the F2H-3 Big Banjo. Carrier qualifications were conducted for nine pilots aboard the USS Bennington (CVA-20) in September and October. The squadron's first deployment was aboard the USS Wasp (CVA-18) from 16 September 1953 through April 1954. Four aircraft were assigned from October until the remainder of the squadron joined the

---

Below, VF-171 aboard the USS Wasp (CVA-18) in 1954. (USN)

ship in January 1954. This was an around-the-world cruise which started with Operation Mariner in the North Atlantic. She then operated in the Med before transiting the Suez Canal and joining Task Force 77 in the South China Sea. In 1954, the ship was visited by Chiang Kai-Shek and President Ramon Magsaysay of the Philippines.

As part of CVG-17, VF-171 deployed aboard the USS Coral Sea (CVA-43) from 4 April through 29 September 1955.

Below, VF-171 F2H-3s aboard the USS Wasp (CVA-18) in March 1954. (National Archives)

VF-171's ENS Dickey crashes his F2H-3, BuNo 126379, aboard CVA-20 on 24 September 1956. (National Archives)

Above, censored VF-171 bird takes the barrier after striking the ramp and sheading its wheels. (via Rich Dan) At left, two VF-71 F2H-3s on the catapults with a VF-171 F2H-3 awaiting its turn, (USN) Below, three VF-171 aircraft during the launch cycle on the USS Coral Sea (CVA-43) on 20 April 1955. The closest F2H-3 has blue tip tanks. (USN)

Carrier qualifications were conducted aboard the USS Bennington (CVA-20) in September 1956 and in October 1956 pilots trained on the

new mirror landing system while aboard the USS Franklin D. Roosevelt (CVA-42). The Suez crises saw FDR with VF-171 aboard operating off Portugal from 7 November through 9 December 1956. The squadron conducted cold weather tests off Maine the week of 18 February 1957 and an aerial demonstration was conducted near Bermuda for President Eisenhower on 21 February. In May 1957, carrier trials were conducted aboard the Navy's new supercarrier, the USS Saratoga (CVA-60). Another deployment was made aboard FDR from 27 July 1957 through 13 February 1958.

The squadron was disestablished on 15 March 1958.

At top right, VF-171 F2H-3 BuNo 126489 traps aboard FDR in 1957. (USN) At right, three VF-171 F2H-3s wait for their turn to launch from CVA-43 with a VF-172 F2H-2 in the foreground. (USN) Below, F4D-1 launches from the USS Franklin D. Roosevelt (CVA-42) as a VF-171 F2H-3 BuNo 126380 approches the catapult. (USN)

FIGHTER SQUADRON ONE NINETY - THREE, VF-193 "GHOST RIDERS"

VF-193 was established at NAS Alameda, CA, in August 1948 around the F8F Bearcat. In the summer of 1950, the unit acquired the F4U Corsair which it deployed with to Korea for two war cruises.

After returning from Korea, the squadron was reformed as a jet fighter squadron, first with F9F-2s in November and then around the F2H-3 in December 1952. At NAS Moffett Field, CA, the CO, CDR D.E. Carr Jr. and the XO LCDR J.J.S. Davis, had their work cut out for them as 90% of the pilots had never flown a jet. Training was further complicated by the fact that VF-193 was to be AIRPAC's first all-weather fighter squadron.

The Ghost Riders departed Alameda with their natural metal F2H-3s aboard the USS Oriskany (CVA-34) on 14 September 1953. First stop was Hawaii where an ORI was conducted. On 5 October, they sailed for the Far East to join Task Force 77. On 2 March, a squadron Banshee broke in two during a ramp strike. The tail dropped onto the fantail and the forward fuselage rolled down the deck in a fireball. Miraculously, the pilot, LT F.J. Repp, was uninjured. The squadron returned to Alameda on 22 April 1954.

In the summer of 1954, CDR Maurice F. Weisner took command of the squadron. During weapons training, most squadron pilots were awarded the coveted "E" for excellence in weapons delivery. A second Oriskany Westpac deployment was made from 2 March through 21 September 1955.

The squadron's last deployment with the F2H-3 was aboard the USS Yorktown (CVA-10) from March through August 1957. For this cruise the unit sported colorfull blue diamond markings. The "Fighting Lady's" cruise took CVG-19 to Hawaii, Guam, Yokosuka, Subic Bay, Sasebo, Iwakuni, Hong Kong, Kobe, Japan and home.

Below, silver VF-193 F2H-3 after landing aboard the USS Oriskany (CVA-34) in 1953. (NMNA)

Above, VF-193 F2H-3 in flight in 1954. (NMNA) Below, six VF-193 F2H-3s aboard CVA-34 in 1953-54. (NMNA)

Above, crash sequence of VF-193 F2H-3 BuNo 126461 after ramp strike by LT F.J. Repp on 2 March 1954 off the coast of Korea. (USN) Below, remains of the tail section found on the fantail. (NMNA)

Upon return to CONUS, the squadron transitioned to the F3H Demon starting in November 1957. The unit received the F-4B Phantom II in 1963 and was redesignated VF-142 on 15 October 1963. The F-4

At left, remains of forward fuselage of F2H-3 BuNo 126393 after LTJG J.R.C. Mitchell put his aircraft into the fantail of CVA-34. He walked away from the crash, went into the Chief's mess and called the bridge to tell them where he was. (via Tailhook) Below, four VF-193 F2H-3s share the deck with Panthers, Cougars and Skyraiders during the CVA-34 1953-54 cruise. (USN)

was flown throughout the Vietnam War transitioning to the F-14A Tomcat in 1974.

At right, VF-193 F2H-3 BuNo 126393 in 1954. Short guy wires were used to lower wings just enough to fit on the hangar deck. (via Tailhook) Below, VF-193 weapons training deployment at China Lake from 3 to 8 January 1955. (USN via Gary Vervar) Bottom, VF-193 F2H-3 being hoisted aboard the USS Oriskany (CVA-34) for the 1953-54 deployment. (NMNA)

Above, VF-193 F2H-3 BuNo 126328 being towed aft for respot aboard the USS Oriskany (CVA-34) in March 1954 in the Philippine Seas. Wing tips were midnight blue and tail stripe was red. (National Archives) Below, VF-193 aircraft aboard Oriskany in 1955. Two aircraft have blue tip tanks and all have a thin blue tail stripe. (Max Bell)

Above, VF-193 F2H-3 goes around a second time before landing aboard the USS Oriskany (CVA-34) in 1955. (USN) At right, tail flash on F2H-3 CAG bird was top-to-bottom red, white, blue and green for the 1955 Oriskany deployment. (USN) Below, twilight launch of VF-193 aircraft from CVA-34 in 1955. (USN)

Four VF-193 F2H-3s BuNos 127541 (B/301), 127521 (B/303), 127540 (B/305), and 127522 (B/307) from CVA-10 in flight in June 1957. Trim on the spines and diamond on the tails were blue. The squadron insignia was just ahead of the intakes. (National Archives)

128

At right, two views of VF-193 F2H-3 B/302 being prepped for a flight from the USS Yorktown (CVA-10) on 26 June 1957. CDR Durhan Jr's name was painted under the canopy rail. The plane captain sits in the cockpit as the pilot conducts his preflight. (National Archives)

Below, VF-193 F2H-3s BuNos 127521 (B/303) and 127516 (B/308) over the Pacific in June 1957. (National

Above, blue-trimmed F2H-3s BuNos 127521 (B/303) and 127516 (B/308) over the Pacific while assigned to CVA-10. (National Archives) Below, the USS Yorktown CVA-10 with CVG-19 on deck pulls into port in 1957. (USN)

FIGHTER SQUADRON ONE NINETY - FOUR, VF-194 "YELLOW DEVILS"

VF-194 was established on 18 May 1955 and took over the insignia of the first VF-194 which was disestablished on 4 May 1955. The new squadron received the F2H-3 in August 1955 at NAS Moffett Field, CA.

LCDR H.P. Streeper was CO of VF-194 for their 1956 deployment as part of CVG-9 aboard the USS Oriskany (CVA-34) from 11 February through 13 June 1956. During "Operation Seahorse", the squadron posted the highest scrores of any special weapons squadron to that

Below, eight VF-194 F2H-3s in flight in 1957 with "N" tail codes and a large chevron stripe accross the wings and fuselage spine. Stripe appears to be black or dark blue covered in white stars. From bottom to top: BuNo 126326 (N/401), 126356 (N/402), 126366 (N/403), 126402 (N/404), 126400 (N/405), 126454 (N/406), (N/407), and (N/408). (NMNA)

date. This was Oriskany's last cruise as a straight deck carrier.

As part of ATG-3 the squadron deployed aboard the USS Kearsarge (CVA-33) from 9 August 1957 through 2 April 1958. During the cruise,

Above, VF-194 F2H-3 BuNo 126387 (N/408) from CVA-34 in 1956. (NMNA) Below, VF-194 F2H-3 N/402 launches from CVA-34 IN 1956. (NMNA) Bottom, VF-194 F2H-3 BuNo 127508 after landing aboard CVA-33 in 1957. (NMNA)

commanded by CDR J.J.S Davis, one squadron aircraft was lost to a cold cat shot and another suffered a landing gear failure on landing. Ports of call for the deployment were Hawaii, Guam, Japan, Philippines and Hong Kong.

After returning from this cruise the squaadron was disestablished on 10 April 1958. However, it carried one F2H-3 on strength through September 1958.

Above, VF-194 F2H-3 BuNo 127509 leaving the angle of CVA-33 in 1957 while assigned to ATG-3. (NMNA) Below, VF-194 F2H-3 BuNo 127534 aboard CVA-33 in 1958 with a VA-26 F9F-8. (via Burger)

Above, VF-194 F2H-3 BuNo 126309 over the Western Pacific in 1958 while assigned to CVA-33. (NMNA) Below, as part of ATG-3 VF-194 F2H-3 BuNo 126485 crosses the fantail of CVA-33. (NMNA) Bottom, VF-194 F2H-3 BuNo 127530 in flight in 1958. Aircraft was trimmed in yellow outlined in black. (NMNA)

FIGHTER SQUADRON TWO - THIRTEEN, VF-213 "BLACK LIONS"

VF-213 was established on 22 June 1955 with four officers and twenty enlisted men at NAS Moffett Field, CA. CDR William Anderson, CO of VF-213 was assigned 29 F2H-3 Banshees with the first arriving the last week of June.

As part of CVG-21, the squadron deployed aboard the USS Bon Homme Richard (CVA-31) for a Western Pacific cruise from 16 August 1956 through 28 February 1957. After returning to CONUS, the Black Lions transitioned to the Douglas F4D-1 in July 1957. Two Skyray deployments later, they started flying the F3H-2 Demon on 14 December 1959.

In February 1964, they received the F-4G Phantom II. The F-14A replaced the Phantoms in December 1976.

Below, VF-213 F2H-3 BuNo 126459 launches from the USS Bon Homme Richard (CVA-31) in February 1957. (NMNA)

Above, VF-213 F2H-3 landing aboard CVA-31 in February 1957. (NMNA) Below, nine VF-213 F2H-3s in flight over the Philippines in December 1956. (NMNA)

F2H-3's

#126396, VF-213, 1956, CVA-31. UPPER SURFACES GULL GREY. LOWER
SURFACES, WING CONTROLL SURFACES AND ELEVATORS WHITE. LETTERING
AND WING-WALK OUTLINE BLACK. LEADING EDGES NATURAL METAL. INTAKE
CHEVRON RED WITH WHITE LETTERING. CANOPY TRIANGLE RED.

#127515, USS BON HOMME RICHARD, VF-213.

#126484, CVA-31, VF-213.

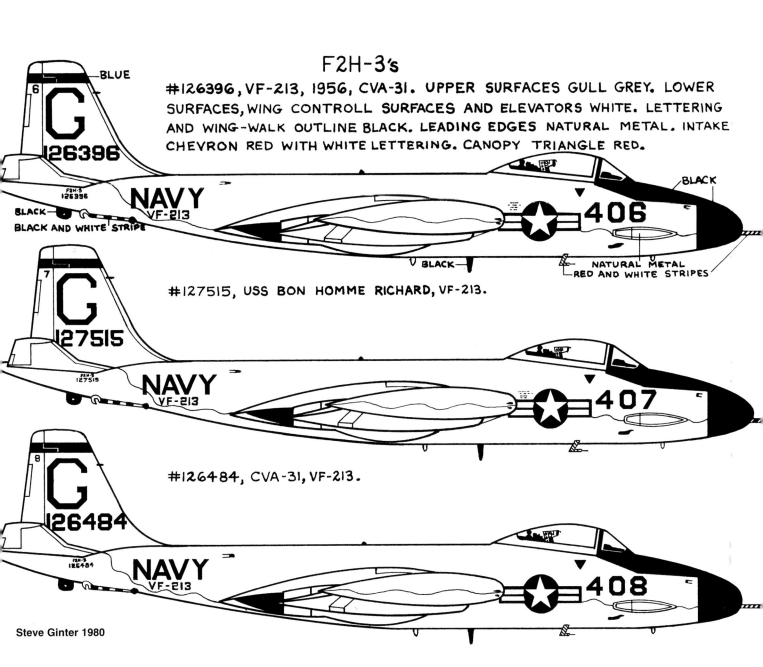

Steve Ginter 1980

F2H-3

#126404. UPPER SURFACES GULL GREY, LOWER SURFACES WHITE, WITH DAY-GLO
MARKINGS. LETTERING BLACK. INTAKE CHEVRON AND CANOPY TRIANGLE RED WITH
WHITE LETTERING. NATURAL METAL LEADING EDGES.

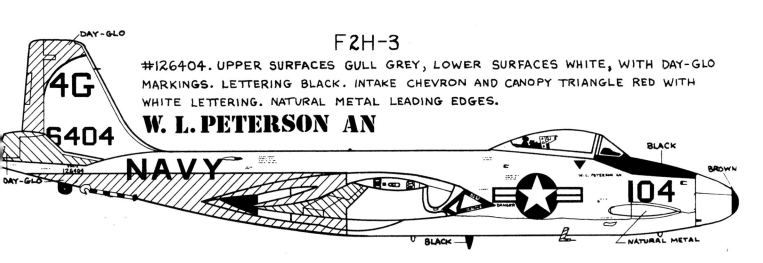

NAVCICOFFSCOL, CIC SCHOOL, NAS GLYNCO

The Naval Combat Information Center Officer School (NAVACI-COFFSCOL) or CIC school at NAS Glynco began receiving F2H-3s in May 1958 with six on-hand on the 31st. As the Big Banjo was retired from the fleet, a large number found their way to the CIC school. The unit topped-out with forty-six F2H-3s and twelve F2H-4s on 30 June 1959. The last Banshee departed Glynco in September 1960.

Below, CIC school F2H-3 BuNo 126404 in 1960 at NAF Litchfield Park. (Harry Gann) Middle, F2H-3 BuNo 127544 on 21 March 1960 at Litchfield Park. (William Swisher) Bottom, ex-CIC school F2H-4s BuNos 127673 and 127651 were assigned to the reserves at NAS Oakland, CA. 673 is missing its engine in this 6 September 1959 photo. All aircraft were trimmed in international orange or da-glo red/orange (William T. Larkins)

RESERVE SQUADRON VF-876 and VF-879 NAS OAKLAND, CA

The Naval Air Reserve Training Unit at NAS Oakland, CA, started receiving Big Banjos in May 1958. Strength at Oakland rose above thirty aircraft which were jointly utilized by VF-876 and VF-879. The only other reserve station to receive the Big Banjos was NAS Norfolk, VA. They acquired twelve aircraft, however there is no evidence they were ever utilized. The last Banshee was retired from Oakland in March 1961.

VF-879, Oakland's first jet fighter squadron, conducted its annual two week Active Duty for Training (ACDU-TRA) for 1959 in June with 21 pilots. Commanded by CDR Ken Friedenbach, the squadron's F2H-3s and TV-2s flew 600 flight hours on sorties throughout the west. These exercises were designed to hone their all-weather skills. In February 1960, the squadron conducted its two week cruise from NAS Miramar, CA. The squadron transitioned to the A4D-1 in December 1960 and moved to NAS Alameda, CA, as VA-879.

VF-876's annual two week Active Duty for Training for 1959 was conducted at home at NAS Oakland, CA. Commanded by CDR Richard J. Scagliotti, 20 pilots, 5 ground officers and 18 enlisted men took part in the training. Each pilot flew an average of forty hours in their F2H-3 Big Banjos concentrating on fighter intercept exercises. Like VF-879, VF-876 transitioned to the A4D-1 and was redesignated VA-876.

Below, NAS Oakland, CA, reserve F2H-3s BuNos 126348 (F/143), 126485 (F/144), 127509 (F/145), and 127534 (F/146) in flight. Tail band was international orange. (Fred Roos collection)

Above, F2H-3 BuNo 126329 at NAS Oakland on 31 August 1958. (William T. Larkins) Below, F2H-3 BuNo 127523 at Oakland on 17 May 1958. (William T. Larkins) Bottom, F2H-4 BuNo 127613 at Oakland on 16 May 1959. (Larry Smalley)

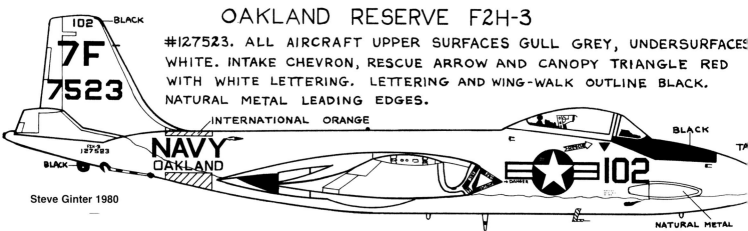

OAKLAND RESERVE F2H-3

#127523. ALL AIRCRAFT UPPER SURFACES GULL GREY, UNDERSURFACES WHITE. INTAKE CHEVRON, RESCUE ARROW AND CANOPY TRIANGLE RED WITH WHITE LETTERING. LETTERING AND WING-WALK OUTLINE BLACK. NATURAL METAL LEADING EDGES.

Steve Ginter 1980

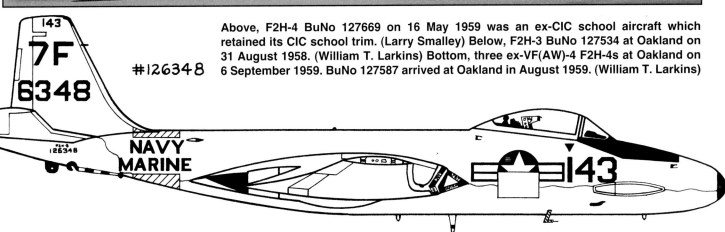

#126348

Above, F2H-4 BuNo 127669 on 16 May 1959 was an ex-CIC school aircraft which retained its CIC school trim. (Larry Smalley) Below, F2H-3 BuNo 127534 at Oakland on 31 August 1958. (William T. Larkins) Bottom, three ex-VF(AW)-4 F2H-4s at Oakland on 6 September 1959. BuNo 127587 arrived at Oakland in August 1959. (William T. Larkins)

Above, four unmarked ex-VF(AW)-4 F2H-4s 127677, 127557, 127620, and 127600 at Oakland with F2H-4 BuNo 127613 on 6 September 1959. The four VF(AW)-4 Banshees arrived at Oakland from NAS Quonset Point in August 1959. (William T. Larkins) Below, one of the ex-VF(AW)-4 F2H-4s with red and white barber pole refueling probe at NAS Oakland. Note Sidewinder missile pylon under the wing. (William T. Larkins)

MARINE FIGHTER SQUADRON ONE-FOURTEEN, VMF-114 "DEATH DEALERS"

VMF-114 was established at MCAS El Toro, CA, in 1943 with the F4U Corsair. In February 1946, the squadron transferred to MCAS Cherry Point, NC, where they operated as a night fighter unit from August 1947 through June 1953 as VMF(N)-114. The squadron then transitioned to the McDonnell F2H-4 Banshee which it flew until replaced by the Grumman F9F-8 Cougar in January 1955.

On 1 May 1957, the squadron was redesignated Marine All-Weather Fighter Squadron One Hundred Fourteen (VMF(AW)-114) and began the transition to the Douglas F4D-1 Skyray. On 1 July 1963, the squadron was disestablished at NAS Atsugi, Japan.

Below, natural metal VMF-114 F2H-4 Banshees in flight. (via Rich Dan)

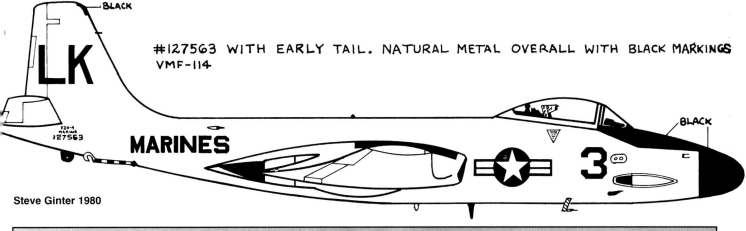

BLACK

#127563 WITH EARLY TAIL. NATURAL METAL OVERALL WITH BLACK MARKINGS
VMF-114

F2H-4
MARINE
127563

MARINES

BLACK

Steve Ginter 1980

Above, VMF-114 F2H-4 BuNo 127647. (Balogh via Menard) Below, VMF-114 F2H-4 BuNo 127647 at MCAS Cherry Point on 24 March 1954. (USMC via Fred Roos)

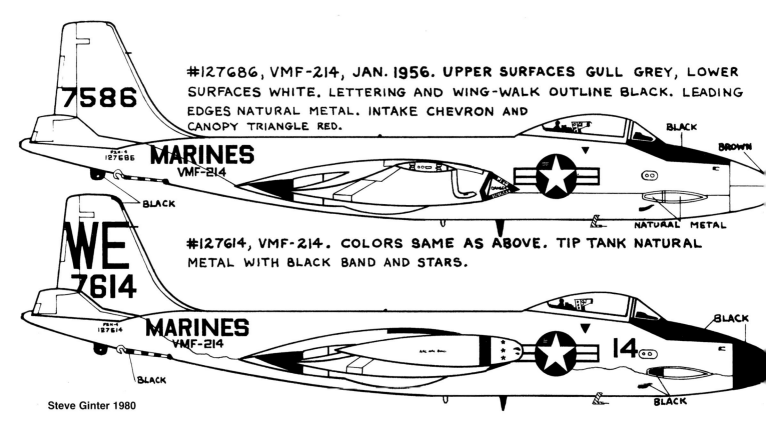

#127686, VMF-214, JAN. 1956. UPPER SURFACES GULL GREY, LOWER SURFACES WHITE. LETTERING AND WING-WALK OUTLINE BLACK. LEADING EDGES NATURAL METAL. INTAKE CHEVRON AND CANOPY TRIANGLE RED.

#127614, VMF-214. COLORS SAME AS ABOVE. TIP TANK NATURAL METAL WITH BLACK BAND AND STARS.

Steve Ginter 1980

MARINE FIGHTER SQUADRON TWO FOURTEEN, VMF-214 "BLACK SHEEP"
MARINE ALL -WEATHER FIGHTER SQUADRON TWO FOURTEEN, VMF(AW)-214
MARINE ATTACK SQUADRON TWO FOURTEEN, VMA-214

VMF-214 was activated on 1 July 1942 at MCAS Ewa, TH, and equipped with Grumman F4F-4 Wildcats. The unit moved to Guadalcanal in March 1943 and transitioned to the Vought F4U-1 Corsair in June. With the new aircraft, the unit became known as the Swashbucklers. After a combat tour in the Russell Islands, the squadron members went to Australia for a little R&R.

Meanwhile, a Major attached to the Air Group borrowed 214's squadron number, obtained aircraft and pilots from the group's personnel pool and formed the most infamous Marine squadron ever, "The Black Sheep". With MAJ Greg "Pappy" Boyington at the helm, the Black Sheep made numerous successful fighter sweeps over Rabaul. In Just 84 days the unit destroyed or damaged 197 enemy aircraft and Pappy's kill record rose to 26. Shortly before the unit rotated back to the US, Boyington was shot down and taken prisoner but was awarded the Congressional Medal of Honor for his actions.

VMF-214 arrived at MCAS Santa Barbara in January 1944 for rest and retraining. They returned to the Pacific theater aboard the USS Franklin (CV-13). The Franklin was bombed and nearly sunk, and the squadron regrouped at MCAAS EL Centro, where it was deactivated. VMF-214 accounted for 127 enemy aircraft shot down.

VMF-214 was reactivated in 1948 and equipped with F4U-4s. The unit moved to Japan in July 1950 and boarded the USS Sicily with F4U-4Bs for operations against North Korea. VMF-214 moved to MCAS Kaneohe Bay, TH, and then MCAS El Toro, CA.

Transition training for the Panther started in late 1951, but due to war losses the first F9F-5s did not arrive until July 1952. 214 moved back to Kaneohe in November and was forced to give up a number of its F9F-5s to the navy to replenish war losses. In return they received 12 war-weary F9F-2s.

In the spring of 1953, while under the command of LTCOL Carr, they

---

VMF-214 F2H-4 BuNo 127586 near San Diego on 19 January 1956. (NAH via Tailhook)

MARINE F2H-4's

EARLY VMF-214 BLACKSHEEP. EARLY TAIL. NATURAL METAL OVERALL WITH BLACK LETTERING AND WING-WALKS. NO TIP TANK PROVISION. CANOPY TRIANGLE WHITE WITH RED LETTERING AND RED OUTLINE.

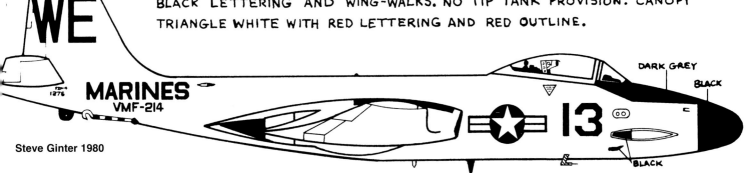

Steve Ginter 1980

145

transitioned to the McDonnell F2H-4 Banshee and were transferred back to El Toro on 27 May. They were redesignated VMF(AW)-214 in December 1956. In 1957, the squadron had the added mission of strip alert in concert with the Hawaiian ANG F-86s at Hickam AFB. The ANG worked the day shift and 114 cover the dusk-to-dawn shift. Day and night carrier qualifications were conducted aboard the USS Yorktown (CVA-10) In March 1957. CO LTCOL Arthur N. Nehf Jr. took his F2H-4s aboard the USS Hancock (CVA-19) as part of ATG-2 from 6 April through 18 September 1957. Nehf had taken over the squadron in January 1956 and had fourteen months to prepare it for sea duty. During the workup the squadron accepted three-out-of-four quarterly AIRFMFPAC safety awards. During the cruise, the unit's mission was to provide close air support, medium-range special weapons delivery and all-weather intercepts.The unit began transitioning to the North American FJ-4B Fury upon their return, and

Above, VMF-214 F2H-4 landing at MCAS Kaneohe, T.H., in 1956. (Howard Fromm) Below, VMF-214 F2H-4 BuNo 127614 at MCAS Kaneohe Bay in March 1956. (Clay Jansson)

were redesignated VMA-214 on 9 July 1957. The last Banshee was retired on 14 March 1958.

The Black Sheep transitioned to the Douglas A4D-2 Skyhawk in

Above, four VMF-214 F2H-3s in flight from CVA-19 in May 1957. BuNos 127586, 127579, 127622 and 127625. (National Archives) Below, VMF-214 natural metal F2H-4 refueling from an AJ-2 Savage tanker aircraft. (Howard Fromm) Bottom, VFP-61 F2H-2P BuNo 125072 escorted by VMF-214 F2H-4 BuNo 127583 while assigned to the USS Hancock (CVA-19) in 1957. (USN)

January 1962. By March 1965, VMA-214 had upgraded to A-4Cs and deployed to Japan. At El Toro they transitioned to the A-4E/F and then the A-4M Skyhawk during the early 1980s. In the late 1980s, the A-4Ms were replaced with AV-8Bs.

Above, VMF-214 F2H-4 aboard CVA-20 on 3 November 1956. (NMNA) Below, VMF-214 F2H-4s aboard CVA-19 in 1957. (NMNA)

MARINE FIGHTER SQUADRON FIVE THIRTY-THREE, VMF-533 "BLACK DIAMONDS"
MARINE ALL -WEATHER FIGHTER SQUADRON FIVE THIRTY - THREE, VMF(AW)-533
MARINE ATTACK SQUADRON FIVE THIRTY - THREE, VMA-533 "NIGHT HAWKS"

VMA-533 was originally established as VMF(N)-533 on 1 October 1943 with F6F-5N night fighters. They were the Marines' third such squadron of night fighters to be organized in WWII. In April 1944, the squadron reached the West Coast and embarked on the USS Long Island (CVE-1). On 6 May the unit arrived at Eniwetok and relieved VMF(N)-532 and assumed the night defense of the area. In November, the squadron moved to Engebi where they stayed until June of 1945 when they transferred to Le Shima. On 14 July, the outfit moved to Chimu on Okinawa where they remained until the war's end. When the war ended, VMF-533 had 35 kills to its credit, more than any other US night fighter squadron.

From October 1945 through January 1947, the squadron remained at Chimu. The squadron transferred in February 1947 to Cherry Point, NC, where they acquired the Grumman F7F Tigercat. During the Korean War, the squadron remained at Cherry Point where they trained all-weather fighter pilots. These pilots were sent to Korea individually upon completion of their training.

After the Korean War, in May 1953, the Tigercats were replaced with the McDonnell F2H-4 Banshee and in June 1955 VMF-533 carrier qualified aboard the USS Lake Champlain (CVA-39). In July, the squadron sent a Detachment aboard the USS Bennington (CVA-20) for a short cruise. In September, VMF-533

Below, the USS Lake Champlain (CVA-39) with VMF-533 embarked. (USN)

At top, VMF-533 F2H-4 during transition training. Note squadron F7F-3N in the background. (via CAPT Rich Dan) Above, VMF-533 F2H-4 BuNo 127549 piloted by MAJ R.H. Hoffman. (via Harry Gann) Below, VMF-533 F2H-4 BuNo 127690 in September 1955. (Doug Olson via Swisher) Bottom, VMF-533 F2H-4 BuNo 127661 at Dayton, OH, in 1954 with refueling probe. (via Bowers)

F2H-4's OF VMF-533

#127549. ALL AIRCRAFT NATURAL METAL. LETTERING, WING-WALK, ANTI-GLARE PANEL BLACK. RADOME TESTORS #1166 FLAT BROWN.

MAJ. R.H. HOFFMAN PILOTS NAME UNDER WINDSCREEN

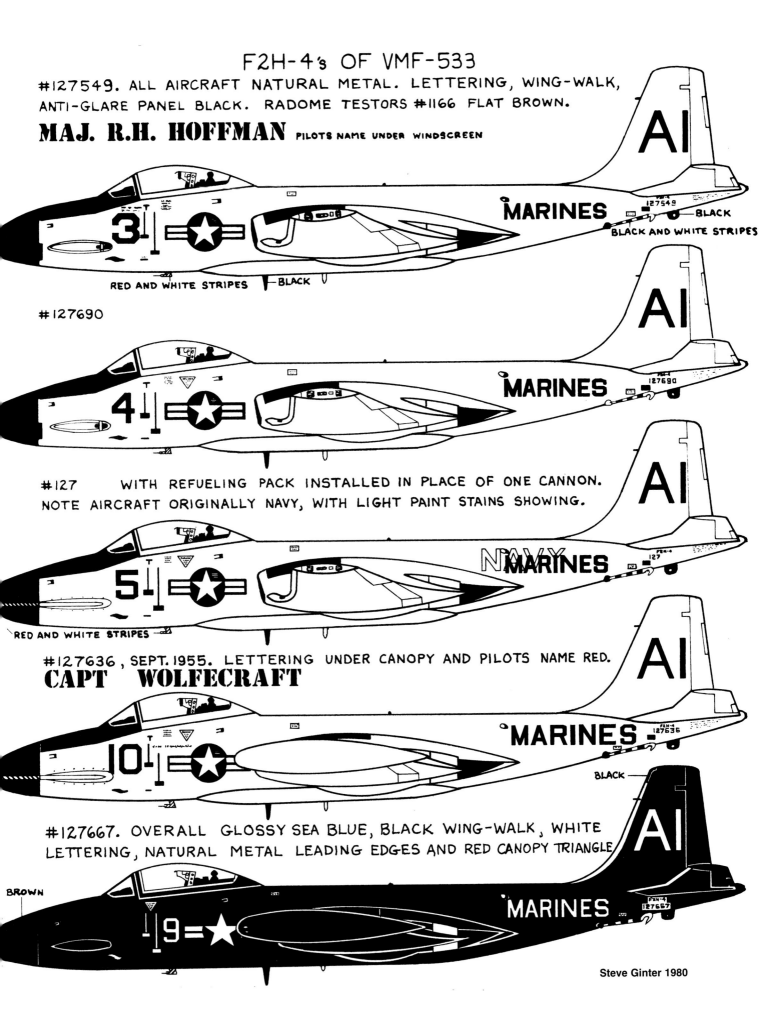

MARINES — BLACK
BLACK AND WHITE STRIPES

RED AND WHITE STRIPES — BLACK

#127690

#127 WITH REFUELING PACK INSTALLED IN PLACE OF ONE CANNON. NOTE AIRCRAFT ORIGINALLY NAVY, WITH LIGHT PAINT STAINS SHOWING.

RED AND WHITE STRIPES

#127636, SEPT. 1955. LETTERING UNDER CANOPY AND PILOTS NAME RED.

CAPT WOLFECRAFT

BLACK

#127667. OVERALL GLOSSY SEA BLUE, BLACK WING-WALK, WHITE LETTERING, NATURAL METAL LEADING EDGES AND RED CANOPY TRIANGLE

BROWN

Steve Ginter 1980

participated in the National Air Show held in Philadelphia, PA.

While under the command of MAJ M.C. Dalby the squadron deployed aboard the Champ from 21 January through August 1957 as part of ATG-182 and was redesignated VMF(AW)-533. Three exercises were conducted during the cruise: Green

Above, natural metal VMF-533 F2H-4 BuNo 127636 with CAPT Wozencraft painted on the forward fuselage. Refueling probe was red and white. (via Dave Menard) Below, VMF(N)-533 F2H-4s BuNos 127675 (AI/1), and 127567 (AI/9) aboard the USS Ticonderoga at Philadelphia for the National Aircraft Show in September 1955. (Fred Roos collection)

Epoch from 13-15 February, Red Pivot from 12-15 April and Rosie-Rosie from 24-28 June. Ports-of-call were Valencia, Naples, Istanbul, Salonika, Athens, Livorno, Barcelona, Cannes, Marseille, Palma De Majorca and Gilbraltar. During the cruise, the squadron was redesignated VMA-533.

In September 1957, with F9F Cougars and designated VMA-533 they boarded the USS F.D. Roosevelt (CVA-42) for carrier qualifications and a short at-sea period lasting through October before transferring to the USS Saratoga (CVA-60) for another two-month at-sea period. In 1957, the squadron deployed twice aboard the USS Lake Champlain. These deployments were from January through July and from September through October. After numerous deployments to Puerto Rico, the squadron traded-in their F-9F-8B's for the Douglas A4D-2 on 19 August 1959. A-4Cs were received in February 1964 and Grumman A-6A Intruders were received on 1 July 1965. They were redesignated VMA(AW)-533 to reflect their new mission and later became VMFA(AW)-533 flying the F/A-18D Hornet.

Above, VMF-533 on CVA-39 in April 1957. Some aircraft have natural metal tip tanks. (National Archives) Below, VMF-533 F2H-4 tanking from a VAH-7 AJ-2 Savage from CVA-39 in April 1957. (National Archives)

Thirty-nine used McDonnell F2H-3 Banshees were purchased from the US Navy for use by the Royal Canadian Navy from November 1955 through September 1962. Three squadrons flew the type: fighter squadron VF-870 (1955-1962), experimental squadron VX-10, and VF-871 (1956-1959). Home-based at Shearwater Naval Air Station, Dartmouth, Nova Scotia, the two fighter squadrons operated from the HMCS Bonaventure.

VF-870 retired its Hawker Sea Furies in 1954 in preparation of the receipt of the F2H-3 Banshee. However, gestation troubles with the F3H Demon prevented the delivery of F2H-3 for over a year. In July 1955, groundcrews began three months of indoctrination training in the United States. Instruction was received at NAS Jacksonville, NAS Cecil Field, MCAS Cherry Point, and NAS Oceana. At the same time nine pilots went to NAS Key West to FAWTU-LANT for airborne intercept training in the F3D Skyknight and in September to VF-41 for conversion training.

On 20 November 1955, the CO, LCDR Bob Falls and three pilots proceeded to NAS Quonset Point, RI, to pick up the first squadron F2H-3s. Two aircraft were ferried to Shearwater on the 25th, two on 4 December, two on the 8th, two on the 12th and two on the 16th. The squadron became more and more proficient and additional training at Key West's FAWTULANT was conducted in 1956, 1957, 1958 and 1959. But it wasn't until September 1957 until the first carrier operations aboard the Bonaventure were accomplished. This was followed by regular carrier operations including a deployment to Ireland. Additional training exercises were conducted in the US including live-fire Sidewinder tests for all pilots. Banshee operations came to a conclusion when the squadron was paid off on 30 September 1962.

VF-871's last Sea Fury flight took place on 31 August 1956, but deliveries of the unit's first Banshees which

was scheduled for 1 September were delayed and four additional F2H-3s were assigned to VF-870 instead and allotted for joint usage by VF-870 and VF-871. Like VF-870, VF-871 pilots received training at Key West before conversion training on the F2H-3 was conducted. The squadron did not receive any of its own aircraft until January 1957. The squadron's first carrier operations did not occur until February 1958. Losses and the difficulty of maintaining a minimum of eight flyable aircraft per squadron led to the paying-off of VF-871 on 16 March 1959.

VX-10 was formed in 1953 with the responsibility for the testing, development, and evaluation of all new aircraft, weapons systems, aircraft design changes, acceptance and overhaul and aircraft-related equipment both ashore and afloat. Canadian Banshees did not usually operate with tip tanks due to their long range and for a very practical reason. The F2H-3 with tip tanks attached could not fit in the hangar deck of the Bonaventure with the wings folded. However VX-10 tested the Big Banjo with tip tanks fitted for all carrier operations. The squadron was disbanded in 1964.

CANADIAN BANSHEE MARKINGS
VF-870:
Late 1955 to late 1956: Nose numbers 100-108, no markings on tip tanks or rudder.

Late 1956 to late 1957: Nose numbers 100-108; if tip tanks were fitted they displayed a red arrow with white outline. Some aircraft had alternating blue and white rudder stripes.

Late 1957 through 1959: Nose numbers 100-108; after March 1959 nose numbers 100-120 after acquiring VF-871 aircraft. If fitted with tip tanks blue noses and red Maple Leaf. Tail had eight blue saw-teeth on a white rudder.

1960 through 1962: Nose numbers were the last three digits of the BuNo, tail and tip tank markings as above.

VF-871:
Nose numbers 140-150; early photos

show no rudder marks, but red and white rudder stripes were soon added. Tip tanks if carried had a black duck painted on them.

VX-10:
Nose numbers 700 and above if carried; no rudder marks, but some aircraft carried a large red "X" on the tail.

BuNos	NOTES
126294	
126295	Was 112 of VF-870, 148 of VF871, 295 of VF-870
126306	Was 103 of VF-870, fatal crash with TBM-3E at Shearwater on 27 August 1957
126310	Crashed into ground at Prospect, NS, on 14 May 1957
126313	Was 104 of VF-870, wings folded in flight, crashed McNab's Island on 31 May 1957
126327	Burnt by crash crews in 1964
126330	Lost on ferry flight to Canada on 22 April 1956
126331	Was 331 of VF-870
126333	Brakes failed on carrier, a/c lost at sea on 4 March 1958
126334	Was 334 of VF-870, preserved in Calgary
126335	Was 335 of VF-870, scrapped in 1963
126337	Was 144 of VF-871, hard landing leading to hangar queen, burnt to train crash crews in 1964
126339	
126343	Was 118 of VF-870, 343 of VF-870
126346	Was 346 of VF-870, scrapped in 1963
126347	
126361	Was 150 of VF-871
126381	Was 700 of VX-10, 149 of VF-871, 381 of VF-870, flew the Atlantic in 1957, scrapped in 1963
126382	Was 382 of VF-870
126390	Was 390 of VF-870, burnt by crash crews in 1964
126392	Was 100 of VF-870, VX-10
126400	Was 110 of VF-870, lost to cold cat shot on 11 November 1959
126402	Was 402 of VF-870, preserved at Shearwater
126403	Lost at sea 2 October 1957
126414	Was 102 of VF-870, 414 of VF-870, fire training 1964
126415	
126422	Was 101 of VF-870, fire training 1964
126428	Crashed at sea on 25 February 1958
126429	Was 145 of VF-871, 429 of VF-870
126434	Was 144 of VF-871, 434 of VF-870
126443	
126444	Was 444 of VF-870, burnt to train crash crews in 1964
126446	Was 108 of VF-870
126449	Was 101 of VF-870, 449 of VF-870
126454	Was 100 of VF-870
126464	Preserved at Ottawa
126469	Was 702 of VX-10, 469 of VF-870, scrapped 1963
126488	Was 105 of VF-870, ditched Key West on 14 January 1959
127510	Was 510 of VF-870

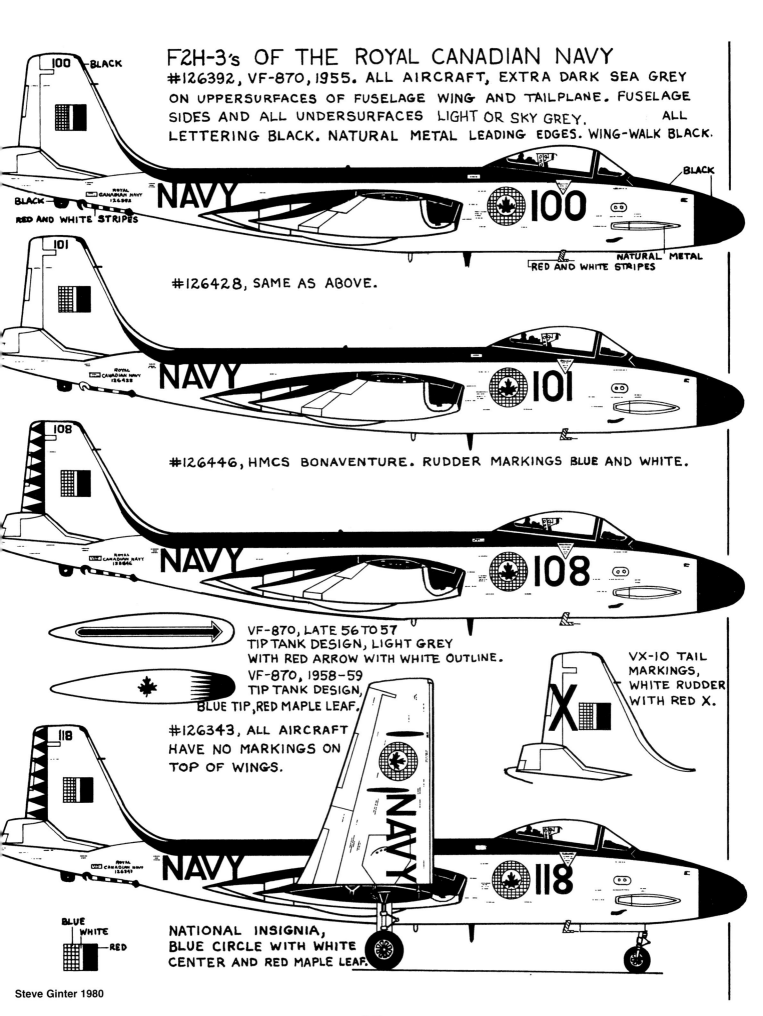

F2H-3's OF THE ROYAL CANADIAN NAVY

#126392, VF-870, 1955. ALL AIRCRAFT, EXTRA DARK SEA GREY ON UPPERSURFACES OF FUSELAGE WING AND TAILPLANE. FUSELAGE SIDES AND ALL UNDERSURFACES LIGHT OR SKY GREY. ALL LETTERING BLACK. NATURAL METAL LEADING EDGES. WING-WALK BLACK.

100 —BLACK

BLACK

RED AND WHITE STRIPES

ROYAL CANADIAN NAVY 126392

NAVY

100

BLACK

RED AND WHITE STRIPES

NATURAL METAL

#126428, SAME AS ABOVE.

101

ROYAL CANADIAN NAVY 126428

NAVY

101

#126446, HMCS BONAVENTURE. RUDDER MARKINGS BLUE AND WHITE.

108

ROYAL CANADIAN NAVY 126446

NAVY

108

VF-870, LATE 56 TO 57
TIP TANK DESIGN, LIGHT GREY
WITH RED ARROW WITH WHITE OUTLINE.

VF-870, 1958-59
TIP TANK DESIGN,
BLUE TIP, RED MAPLE LEAF.

#126343, ALL AIRCRAFT
HAVE NO MARKINGS ON
TOP OF WINGS.

VX-10 TAIL
MARKINGS,
WHITE RUDDER
WITH RED X.

X

118

ROYAL CANADIAN NAVY 126343

NAVY

NAVY

118

BLUE
WHITE
RED

NATIONAL INSIGNIA,
BLUE CIRCLE WITH WHITE
CENTER AND RED MAPLE LEAF.

Steve Ginter 1980

Above, VF-870 F2H-3 BuNo 126392 flown by squadron CO LCDR Bob Falls on 4 July 1956 in flight over the Halifax bridge. (NMNA) Below, 126392 underside detail as it banks away from the camera plane. (NMNA)

Formation flights of VF-870 F2H-3s on 7 February 1956. BuNos 126392 (100), 126414 (102), 126306 (103), and 126313 (104). (RCN and McDonnell)

Above, VF-870 F2H-3 BuNo 126306 in early 1956 prior to blue and white rudder stripes being applied. (RCN) Below, VF-870 visits the McDonnell plant on 9 September. Nine aircraft were assigned to VF-870, nose numbers 100-108. BuNos 126392 (100), 126422 (101), 126414 (102), 126306 (103), 126313 (104) and 126331 (106). (McDonnell)

Above, VF-870 F2H-3 BuNo 126313 in 1956 with peeling paint on the vertical tail. (Peter M. Bowers) Below, FAWTULANT flight-line at Boca Chica Field, Key West, FL, in February 1957 with seven Canadian Banjos and nine VF-22 Banjos. Also, there are eight FAWTULANT SkyKnights and a TV-2 plus three blimps. (USN) Bottom, two close-up views of the Canadian flightline on 16 May 1957 with BuNo 126392 (100) in the foreground of one and 126414 (104) in the foreground of the second one. Blue and white stripes have been added to the rudder and the squadron badge was applied to the nose. (USN)

Above, VF-870 F2H-3 BuNo 126343 with blue triangles on a white rudder and a Sidewinder under the right wing. (RCN) Below, Sidewinder-armed VF-870 F2H-3 BuNo 126295 inverted over Shearwater in June 1959. (RCN) The planned usage of the Sidewinder on the F2H-3s allowed this second-string interceptor to be viable into 1961.

At top left, VF-870 BuNo 126346 on catapult. (RCN) At left, armorer works on Sidewinder on a VF-870 F2H-3 while sitting on the catapult. (via B. Macleod) Above, LCDR A.E. Fox poses with a Sidewinder. (via B. Macleod) Below, VF-870 created a four-plane aerial demonstration team named the "Grey Ghosts", seen here over the Bonaventure. (RCN)

Above, like VF-870, VF-871 F2H-3s did not initially have rudder markings. BuNo 126429 is also seen at right in company with a former squadron Sea Fury. CO of VF-871, LCDR Bob Laider, was the Banshee pilot and LT Benny Oxholm was piloting the Sea Fury. (RCN) Bottom, VF-871 F2H-3 BuNo 126381 in flight with the squadron's red and white rudder stripes. (RCN)

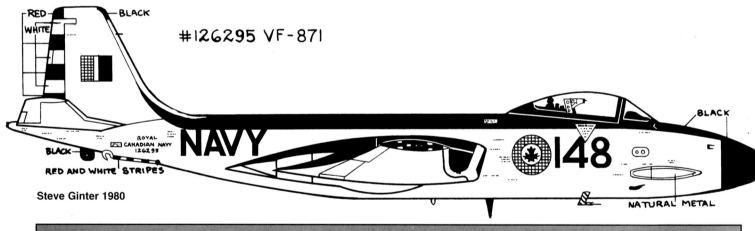

#126295 VF-871

RED
WHITE
BLACK
BLACK
ROYAL CANADIAN NAVY 126295
RED AND WHITE STRIPES
NAVY
148
BLACK
NATURAL METAL

Steve Ginter 1980

In 1960, VF-870 F2H-3s used the last three digits of their BuNos as nose numbers. At top, VF-870 F2H-3 BuNo 126294 with 5" rockets mounted beneath its wings. (Ginter collection) Above, VF-870 F2H-3 BuNo 126382 with wings folded. (Ginter collection) Above right, VF-870 F2H-3 BuNo 126295 in flight with two other McDonnell products, the F-4B Phantom II and the F3H Demon on 3 August 1963. (USN) At right, VX-10 F2H-3 BuNo 126381 aboard Bonaventure. (RCN) Below, VF-870 F2H-3 BuNo 126331 with tip tanks conducting bombing practice with 500 pounders at the Shilo range. (RCN)

Above, F2H-3 BuNo 126402 on display at Shearwater in VF-870 markings. (Ginter collection) Below, F2H-3 BuNo 126464 at Ottawa on 26 July 1972. (O'Dell via Menard) Bottom, BuNo 126464 after restoration in 1987. 464 was one of the four aircraft assigned to the Grey Ghost flight demonstration team. (Ginter collection)

NAVY ALLOWCATION AND LOCATION LISTS FOR THE F2H-3/4 BIG BANJO

What follows is a listing of F2H-3/4 Banshees on strength by month from the Navy Allocation and Location Lists. Months that were unavailable or unreadable were: April 1953, June 1953, January 1954, October 1954, February 1957, December 1958, and October 1959. The reports are only a snapshot in time and only reflect aircraft on hand on the last day of each month. They are not infallable for many reasons. For one thing, Bureau's records are dependent on receipt of reports in time for inclusion. Also, aircraft which have been wrecked, lost or worn out in service are included until officially stricken from the navy list; it is impossible to show the actual status of the aircraft on any given date. NATC aircraft and various R&D aircraft locations have not been included here.

30 NOV 1952

VC-3	Moffett	F2H-3 (9)
VX-3	Atlantic City	F2H-3 (2)
VC-4	Atlantic City	F2H-3 (11)

31 DEC 1952

VC-3	Moffett	F2H-3 (14)
VX-3	Atlantic City	F2H-3 (5)
VC-4	Atlantic City	F2H-3 (12)

31 JAN 1953

VC-3	Moffett	F2H-3 (20)
VX-3	Atlantic City	F2H-3 (7)
VC-4	Atlantic City	F2H-3 (14)

28 FEB 1953

VC-3	Moffett	F2H-3 (20)
VX-3	Atlantic City	F2H-3 (7)
VC-4	Atlantic City	F2H-3 (25)
VF-71	Quonset	F2H-3 (1)
VF-171	Gitmo	F2H-3 (12)
VF-193	Moffitt	F2H-3 (12)

31 MAR 1953

VC-3	Moffett	F2H-3 (20)
VX-3	Atlantic City	F2H-3 (7)
VC-4	Atlantic City	F2H-3 (21)
Det 6	Coral Sea	F2H-3 (5)
VF-23	Moffett	F2H-3 (12)
VF-31	Cecil	F2H-3 (17)
VF-72	Quonset	F2H-3 (1)
VF-141	Miramar	F2H-3 (12)
VF-171	Gitmo	F2H-3 (12)
VF-193	Moffitt	F2H-3 (12)

31 MAY 1953

VC-3	Moffett	F2H-3 (20)
VX-3	Atlantic City	F2H-3 (7)
VC-4	Atlantic City	F2H-3 (25)
Det 6	Coral Sea	F2H-3 (7)
Det 7	F.D.R.	F2H-3 (3)
VF-11	Jacksonville	F2H-3 (1), F2H-4 (11)
VF-23	Moffett	F2H-3 (11)
VF-31	Cecil	F2H-3 (12)
VF-141	Miramar	F2H-3 (12)
VF-171	Gitmo	F2H-3 (16)
VF-193	Moffitt	F2H-3 (13)

FASRONS:

7	San Diego	F2H-3 (3)
10	Moffett	F2H-3 (1)

USMC:

VMA-211	Cherry Pt.	F2H-4 (1)
VMF-214	Kaneohe	F2H-4 (12)

31 JUL 1953

VC-3	Moffett	F2H-3 (12), F2H-4 (3)
Unit A	Yorktown	F2H-3 (4)
Unit C	Kearsarge	F2H-3 (4)
VX-3	Atlantic City	F2H-3 (7)
VC-4	Atlantic City	F2H-3 (13), F2H-4 (20)
Det 6	Coral Sea	F2H-3 (4)
Det 7	F.D.R.	F2H-3 (4)
VF-23	Moffett	F2H-3 (12)
VF-31	Cecil	F2H-3 (12)
VF-41	Oceana	F2H-3 (10)
VF-71	Gitmo	F2H-3 (15)
VF-141	Miramar	F2H-3 (12)
VF-171	Jacksonville	F2H-3 (15)
VF-193	Moffitt	F2H-3 (13)

FASRONS:

7	San Diego	F2H-3 (2)

USMC:

VMF-114	Cherry Pt.	F2H-4 (21)
VMF-214	El Toro	F2H-4 (23)
VMF-533	Cherry Pt.	F2H-4 (23)

31 AUG 53

VC-3	Moffett	F2H-3 (11), F2H-4 (3)
Unit A	Yorktown	F2H-3 (5)
Unit C	Kearsarge	F2H-3 (4)
VX-3	Atlantic City	F2H-3 (6), F2H-4 (2)
VC-4	Atlantic City	F2H-3 (6), F2H-4 (31)
Det 6	Coral Sea	F2H-3 (4)
Det 7	F.D.R.	F2H-3 (4)
Det 38	Wasp	F2H-3 (4)
Det 41	Quonset Pt.	F2H-4 (4)
VF-23	Moffett	F2H-3 (12)
VF-31	Jacksonville	F2H-3 (13)
VF-41	Oceana	F2H-3 (12)
VF-71	Quonset Pt.	F2H-3 (12)
VF-141	Miramar	F2H-3 (12)
VF-171	Jacksonville	F2H-3 (15)
VF-193	Oriskany	F2H-3 (14)

FASRONS:

2	Quonset Pt.	F2H-3 (3)

USMC:

HEDRON	Miami	F2H-4 (2)
HEDRON	El Toro	F2H-4 (3)
VMF-114	Cherry Pt.	F2H-4 (23)
VMF-214	El Toro	F2H-4 (24)
VMF-533	Cherry Pt.	F2H-4 (24)

30 SEP 1953

VC-3	Moffett	F2H-3 (18), F2H-4 (2)
Unit A	Yorktown	F2H-3 (4)
Unit C	Kearsarge	F2H-3 (4)
Unit E	Oriskany	F2H-3 (3)
VX-3	Atlantic City	F2H-3 (6), F2H-4 (2)
VC-4	Atlantic City	F2H-3 (4), F2H-4 (30)
Det 6	Coral Sea	F2H-3 (3)
Det 7	F.D.R.	F2H-3 (4)
Det 38	Wasp	F2H-3 (4)
Det 41	Quonset Pt.	F2H-3 (2), F2H-4 (4)
VX-5	Moffett	F2H-3 (3)
VF-23	Moffett	F2H-3 (14)
VF-31	Jacksonville	F2H-3 (15)
VF-41	Oceana	F2H-3 (15)

(continued)

VF-71	Bennington	F2H-3 (12)
VF-141	Miramar	F2H-3 (15)
VF-171	Bennington	F2H-3 (12)
VF-193	Oriskany	F2H-3 (15)

FASRONS:

2	Quonset Pt.	F2H-3 (3)

USMC:

MARS-37	Miami	F2H-4 (2)
VMF-114	Cherry Pt.	F2H-4 (24)
VMF-214	El Toro	F2H-4 (24)
VMF-533	Cherry Pt.	F2H-4 (24)

31 OCT 1953

VC-3	Moffett	F2H-3 (24), F2H-4 (2)
Unit A	Yorktown	F2H-3 (4)
Unit C	Kearsarge	F2H-3 (4)
Unit E	Oriskany	F2H-3 (4)
VX-3	Atlantic City	F2H-3 (6), F2H-4 (2)
VC-4	Atlantic City	F2H-3 (4), F2H-4 (32)
Det 7	F.D.R.	F2H-3 (4)
Det 38	Wasp	F2H-3 (4)
Det 41	Quonset Pt.	F2H-3 (2), F2H-4 (4)
VF-23	Essex	F2H-3 (14)
VF-31	Key West	F2H-3 (16)
VF-41	Oceana	F2H-3 (16)
VF-71	Bennington	F2H-3 (11)
VF-141	Miramar	F2H-3 (16)
VF-171	Wasp*	F2H-3 (4)
	Bennington	F2H-3 (9)
VF-193	Oriskany	F2H-3 (12)
FAWTU	Key West	F2H-4 (2)

FASRONS:

2	Quonset Pt.	F2H-3 (3)

USMC:

HEDRON	El Toro	F2H-4 (3)
VMF-114	Cherry Pt.	F2H-4 (24)
VMF-214	El Toro	F2H-4 (24)
VMF-533	Cherry Pt.	F2H-4 (24)

30 NOV 1953

VC-3	Moffett	F2H-3 (16)
Unit A	Yorktown	F2H-3 (3)
Unit C	Kearsarge	F2H-3 (4)
Unit E	Oriskany	F2H-3 (4)
Unit I	Essex	F2H-3 (4)
Det 38	Wasp	F2H-3 (1)
VX-3	Atlantic City	F2H-3 (4), F2H-4 (2)
Det 5	Midway	F2H-3 (2)
VC-4	Atlantic City	F2H-3 (1), F2H-4 (32)
Det 32	Tarawa	F2H-4 (4)
Det 38	Wasp	F2H-3 (3)
Det 41	Quonset Pt.	F2H-3 (2), F2H-4 (3)
VF-23	Essex	F2H-3 (12)
VF-31	Midway	F2H-3 (15)
VF-41	Oceana	F2H-3 (16)
VF-71	Bennington	F2H-3 (14)
VF-141	Miramar	F2H-3 (15)
VF-152	Moffett	F2H-3 (12)
VF-171	Wasp*	F2H-3 (4)
	Bennington	F2H-3 (7)
VF-193	Oriskany	F2H-3 (12)
FAWTU	Key West	F2H-4 (18)
FAGU	El Centro	F2H-3 (5)

FASRONS:

2	Quonset Pt.	F2H-3 (3)
10	Moffett	F2H-3 (2)
104	Pt. Lyautry	F2H-3 (2)

USMC:

HEDRON	El Toro	F2H-4 (3)
VMF-114	Cherry Pt.	F2H-4 (24)
VMF-214	El Toro	F2H-4 (24)
VMF-533	Cherry Pt.	F2H-4 (24)

31 DEC 1953

VC-3	Moffett	F2H-3 (17)

Unit A	Yorktown	F2H-3 (3)
Unit B	Oriskany	F2H-3 (4)
Unit I	Essex	F2H-3 (3)
Det 38	Wasp	F2H-3 (2)
VX-3	Atl. City	F2H-3 (2), F2H-4 (2)
Det 5	Midway	F2H-3 (2)
VC-4	Quonset	F2H-4 (7)
Det 38	Wasp	F2H-3 (2)
VF-11	Cecil	F2H-4 (10)
VF-23	Essex	F2H-3 (11)
VF-31	Midway	F2H-3 (15)
VF-41	Oceana	F2H-3 (16)
VF-71	Bennington	F2H-3 (11)
VF-141	Miramar	F2H-3 (13)
VF-152	Moffett	F2H-3 (12)
VF-171	Wasp*	F2H-3 (5)
FAWTU	Key West	F2H-4 (1)
FASRONS:		
2	Quonset Pt.	F2H-3 (6)
5	Oceana	F2H-4 (2)
6	Jacksonville	F2H-3 (2)
11	Atsugi	F2H-3 (3)
104	Pt. Lyauty	F2H-3 (2), F2H-4 (1)
USMC:		
MTG-20	Cherry Pt.	F2H-4 (3)
MARS-37	Miami	F2H-4 (3)
VMF-114	Cherry Pt.	F2H-4 (24)
VMF-214	El Toro	F2H-4 (26)
VMF-533	Cherry Pt.	F2H-4 (24)

28 FEB 1954

VC-3	Moffett	F2H-3 (22)
Det E	Oriskany	F2H-4 (3)
Det I	Essex	F2H-3 (3)
Det 38	Wasp	F2H-3 (3)
Det 54	Randolph	F2H-4 (3)
VX-3	Atlantic City	F2H-3 (4)
VC-4	Atlantic City	F2H-3 (3), F2H-4 (35)
Det 4	Bennington	F2H-3 (1)
VX-5	Moffett	F2H-3 (3)
VF-11	Cecil	F2H-4 (9), F3D-2 (1)
VF-23	Essex	F2H-3 (11)
VF-31	Midway	F2H-3 (12)
VF-41	GITMO/Horn.	F2H-3 (16)
VF-71	Bennington	F2H-3 (11)
VF-141	Randolph	F2H-3 (12)
VF-152	Moffett	F2H-3 (13)
VF-171	Wasp	F2H-3 (12)
VF-193	Oriskany	F2H-3 (12)
FASRONS:		
2	Quonset Pt.	F2H-3 (6)
4	San Diego	F2H-3 (6), F2H-4 (3)
5	Oceana	F2H-3 (4), F2H-4 (1)
10	Moffett	F2H-3 (3), F2H-4 (1)
12	Miramar	F2H-3 (1)
104	Pt. Lyauty	F2H-3 (2)
117	Barbers Pt.	F2H-3 (2)
120	Iwakuni	F2H-3 (13)
USMC:		
MTG-20	Cherry Pt.	F2H-4 (4)
VMF-114	Cherry Pt.	F2H-4 (24)
VMF-214	El Toro	F2H-4 (24)
VMF-533	Cherry Pt.	F2H-4 (24)

31 MAR 1954

VC-3	Moffett	F2H-3 (22)
Det E	Oriskany	F2H-3 (3)
Det I	Essex	F2H-3 (3)
Det 36	Randolph	F2H-3 (4)
Det 40	Wasp	F2H-3 (3)
VX-3	Atlantic City	F2H-3 (4)
VC-4	Atlantic City	F2H-4 (35), F2H-3 (1)
VX-5	Moffett	F2H-4 (3)
VF-11	Cecil	F2H-4 (12)
VF-23	Essex	F2H-3 (12)
VF-31	Midway	F2H-3 (12)
VF-41	Hornet	F2H-3 (16)
VF-71	Bennington	F2H-3 (10)
VF-141	Randolph	F2H-3 (12)
VF-152	Moffett	F2H-3 (12)
VF-171	Wasp	F2H-3 (11)
VF-193	Oriskany	F2H-3 (8)
NADU	S. Weymouth	F2H-4 (2)
NASWF	Kirtland AFB	F2H-3 (2)
NOTS	Inyokern	F2H-3 (1)
FASRONS:		
2	Quonset	F2H-3 (6)
5	Oceana	F2H-3 (2)
6	Jacksonville	F2H-3 (5), F2H-4 (1)
10	Moffett	F2H-3 (7), F2H-4 (1)
11	Atsugi	F2H-3 (10)
12	Miramar	F2H-3 (1)
120	Iwakuni	F2H-3 (5)
USMC		
VMF-114	Cherry Pt.	F2H-4 (24)
VMF-214	Kaneohe	F2H-4 (23)
VMF-533	Cherry Pt.	F2H-4 (24)

30 APR 1954

VC-3	Moffett	F2H-3 (22)
Det I	Essex	F2H-3 (3)
Det H	Hornet	F2H-3 (4)
Det 36	Randolph	F2H-3 (4)
Det 40	Wasp	F2H-3 (3)
VX-3	Atlantic City	F2H-3 (4)
VC-4	Atlantic City	F2H-4 (35)
VX-5	Moffett	F2H-3 (2)
VF-11	Cecil	F2H-4 (12)
VF-23	Essex	F2H-3 (12)
VF-31	Midway	F2H-3 (9)
VF-41	Oceana	F2H-3 (13)
VF-71	Bennington	F2H-3 (12)
VF-141	Randolph	F2H-3 (12)
VF-152	Moffett	F2H-3 (12)
VF-171	Wasp	F2H-3 (11)
VF-193	Moffett	F2H-3 (10)
FASRONS:		
2	Quonset	F2H-3 (4)
3	Norfolk	F2H-4 (1)
4	San Diego	F2H-3 (4)
6	Jacksonville	F2H-3 (4), F2H-4 (1)
10	Moffett	F2H-3 (7), F2H-4 (1)
11	Atsugi	F2H-3 (5)
120	Iwakuni	F2H-3 (8)
USMC		
HEDRON 27	Cherry Pt.	F2H-4 (1)
VMF-114	Cherry Pt.	F2H-4 (22)
VMF-214	Kaneohe	F2H-4 (24)
VMF-533	Cherry Pt.	F2H-4 (24)

31 MAY 1954

VC-3	Moffett	F2H-3 (22)
Det I	Essex	F2H-3 (3)
Det H	Hornet	F2H-3 (4)
Det 36	Randolph	F2H-3 (4)
Det 40	Wasp	F2H-3 (3)
VX-3	Atlantic City	F2H-3 (4)
VC-4	Atlantic City	F2H-3 (2), F2H-4 (34)
VX-5	Moffett	F2H-4 (4)
VF-11	Coral Sea	F2H-4 (11)
VF-23	Essex	F2H-3 (11)
VF-31	Midway	F2H-3 (8)
VF-41	Oceana	F2H-3 (13)
VF-71	Bennington	F2H-3 (11)
VF-141	Randolph	F2H-3 (12)
VF-152	Moffett	F2H-3 (13)
VF-171	Jacksonville	F2H-3 (12)
VF-193	Moffett	F2H-3 (10)
NAF	Opama	F2H-3 (4)

FASRONS:		
4	San Diego	F2H-3 (1)
6	Jacksonville	F2H-4 (1)
10	Moffett	F2H-3 (5), F2H-4 (3)
11	Atsugi	F2H-3 (4)
104	Pt. Lyauty	F2H-4 (1)
USMC		
HEDRON 27	Cherry Pt.	F2H-4 (1)
VMF-114	Cherry Pt.	F2H-4 (24)
VMF-214	Kaneohe	F2H-4 (24)
VMF-533	Cherry Pt.	F2H-4 (24)

30 JUN 1954

VC-3	Moffett	F2H-3 (22)
Det 36	Randolph	F2H-3 (4)
Unit I	Essex	F2H-3 (3)
Unit M	Hornet	F2H-3 (4)
VX-3	Atlantic City	F2H-3 (2), F2H-4 (2)
VC-4	Atlantic City	F2H-4 (35)
VF-11	Cecil	F2H-4 (12)
VF-23	Essex	F2H-3 (12)
VF-31	Midway	F2H-3 (7)
VF-41	Oceana	F2H-3 (12)
VF-71	Bennington	F2H-3 (11)
VF-141	Miramar	F2H-3 (12)
VF-152	Moffett	F2H-3 (12)
VF-171	Jacksonville	F2H-3 (12)
VF-193	Moffett	F2H-3 (10)
NAOTS	Chincoteague	F2H-3 (1)
NOTS	Inyokern	F2H-3 (1)
NASWF	Kirtland	F2H-3 (2)
NADU	S. Weymouth	F2H-4 (2)
BAR R&D	Baltimore	F2H-3 (2)
R&D	St. Louis	F2H-3 (2)
INN	Boston	F2H-3 (1)
FASRONS:		
2	Quonset Pt.	F2H-3 (6)
5	Oceana	F2H-4 (5)
6	Jacksonvile	F2H-3 (1)
10	Moffett	F2H-3 (6), F2H-4 (3)
11	Atsugi	F2H-3 (4)
104	Pt. Lyautey	F2H-3 (2), F2H-4 (1)
USMC:		
VMF-114	Cherry Pt.	F2H-4 (23)
VMF-214	Kaneohe	F2H-4 (23)
VMF-533	Cherry Pt.	F2H-4 (24)

31 JUL 1954

VC-3	Moffett	F2H-3 (22)
Det I	Essex	F2H-3 (3)
Det M	Hornet	F2H-3 (4)
VX-3	Atlantic City	F2H-3 (3), F2H-4 (2)
VC-4	Atlantic City	F2H-4 (35)
VX-5	Moffett	F2H-3 (3)
VF-11	Cecil	F2H-4 (12)
VF-23	Essex	F2H-3 (12)
VF-31	Midway	F2H-3 (7)
VF-41	Oceana	F2H-3 (12)
VF-71	Bennington	F2H-3 (11)
VF-141	Randolph	F2H-3 (12)
VF-152	Moffett	F2H-3 (12)
VF-171	Jacksonville	F2H-3 (12)
VF-193	Moffett	F2H-3 (10)
NAF	Opama	F2H-3 (4)
FASRONS:		
2	Quonset Pt.	F2H-3 (6)
4	San Diego	F2H-3 (1)
5	Oceana	F2H-3 (5)
6	Jacksonville	F2H-3 (1)
10	Moffett	F2H-3 (5), F2H-4 (3)
11	Atsugi	F2H-4 (1)
104	Pt. Lyautry	F2H-4 (1)
117	Barbers Pt.	F2H-4 (2)
USMC		

VMF-114 Cherry Pt. F2H-4 (24)
VMF-214 Kaneohe F2H-4 (24)
VMF-533 Cherry Pt. F2H-4 (24)

31 AUG 1954

VC-3 Moffett F2H-3 (20)
Det H Wasp F2H-3 (4)
Det M Hornet F2H-3 (4)
VX-3 Atlantic City F2H-3 (1), F2H-4 (2)
VC-4 Atlantic City F2H-4 (28)
Det 34 L. Champlain F2H-4 (4)
VX-5 Moffett F2H-3 (3)
VF-11 Coral Sea F2H-4 (12)
VF-23 Moffett F2H-3 (12)
VF-31 Cecil F2H-3 (4)
VF-41 Oceana F2H-3 (10)
VF-71 Key West F2H-3 (13)
VF-141 Miramar F2H-3 (11)
VF-152 Yorktown F2H-3 (12)
VF-171 Jacksonville F2H-3 (15)
VF-193 Moffett F2H-3 (10)
FASRONS:
2 Quonset Pt. F2H-3 (4)
4 San Diego F2H-3 (3)
5 Oceana F2H-3 (4)
10 Moffett F2H-3 (7)
11 Atsugi F2H-3 (8)
104 Pt. Lyauty F2H-3 (1), F2H-4 (1)
117 Barbers Pt. F2H-3 (1)
USMC
HEDRON 27 Cherry Pt. F2H-4 (2)
VMF-114 Cherry Pt. F2H-4 (22)
VMF-214 Kaneohe F2H-4 (25)
VMF-533 Cherry Pt. F2H-4 (23)

30 SEP 1954

VC-3 Moffett F2H-3 (17)
Det H Wasp F2H-3 (4)
Det M Hornet F2H-3 (4)
VX-3 Atlantic City F2H-3 (2), F2H-4 (2)
VC-4 Atlantic City F2H-4 (7)
Det A Leeward Pt. F2H-4 (19)
Det 34 L. Champlain F2H-4 (4)
VX-5 Moffett F2H-3 (2)
VF-11 Coral Sea F2H-4 (11)
VF-23 Moffett F2H-3 (12)
VF-31 Cecil F2H-3 (5)
VF-41 Oceana F2H-3 (13)
VF-71 Key West F2H-3 (9)
VF-141 Miramar F2H-3 (15)
VF-152 Yorktown F2H-3 (11)
VF-171 Key West F2H-3 (13)
VF-193 Moffett F2H-3 (10)
FASRONS:
2 Quonset Pt. F2H-3 (2)
6 Jacksonville F2H-4 (3)
11 Atsugi F2H-3 (4)
104 Pt. Lyauty F2H-3 (1), F2H-4 (1)
117 Barbers Pt. F2H-4 (2)
USMC
VMF-114 Cherry Pt. F2H-4 (24)
VMF-214 Kaneohe F2H-4 (23)
VMF-533 Cherry Pt. F2H-4 (21)

30 NOV 1954

VC-3 Moffett F2H-3 (11)
Det A Essex F2H-3 (4)
Det C Kearsarge F2H-3 (7)
Det H Wasp F2H-3 (4)
Det M Hornet F2H-3 (1)
VX-3 Atlantic City F2H-3 (2), F2H-4 (2)
VC-4 Atlantic City F2H-4 (16)
Det 33 Intrepid F2H-4 (6)
Det 34 L. Champlain F2H-4 (4)
Det 35 Midway F2H-4 (4)

VX-5 Moffett F2H-3 (2)
VF-11 Coral Sea F2H-4 (12)
VF-23 Moffett F2H-3 (12)
VF-31 Cecil F2H-3 (13)
VF-41 Oceana F2H-3 (12)
VF-71 Quonset Pt. F2H-3 (8)
VF-141 Miramar F2H-3 (15)
VF-152 Yorktown F2H-3 (11)
VF-171 Jacksonville F2H-3 (11)
VF-193 Moffett F2H-3 (12)
FASRONS:
2 Quonset Pt. F2H-3 (2)
4 San Diego F2H-4 (2)
5 Oceana F2H-3 (2)
6 Jacksonville F2H-3 (2)
11 Atsugi F2H-3 (3)
104 Pt. Lyauty F2H-3 (1)
USMC
VMF-114 Cherry Pt. F2H-4 (18)
VMF-214 Kaneohe F2H-4 (24)
VMF-533 Cherry Pt. F2H-4 (19)

31 DEC 1954

VC-3 Moffett F2H-3 (15)
Det A Essex F2H-3 (4)
Det C Kearsarge F2H-3 (7)
Det H Wasp F2H-3 (3)
VX-3 Atlantic City F2H-3 (2), F2H-4 (2)
VC-4 Atlantic City F2H-4 (15)
Det 34 L. Champlain F2H-4 (5)
Det 35 Midway F2H-4 (4)
VF-11 Cecil F2H-4 (11)
VF-23 Moffett F2H-3 (11)
VF-31 Cecil F2H-3 (7)
VF-41 Randolph F2H-3 (12)
VF-71 Quonset Pt. F2H-3 (8)
VF-141 Miramar F2H-3 (15)
VF-152 Yorktown F2H-3 (12)
VF-171 Jacksonville F2H-3 (11)
VF-193 Moffett F2H-3 (11)
FASRONS:
11 Atsugi F2H-3 (2)
4 San Diego F2H-3 (5), F2H-4 (2)
104 Pt. Lyauty F2H-3 (1), F2H-4 (1)
USMC
VMF-114 Cherry Pt. F2H-4 (18)
VMF-214 Kaneohe F2H-4 (24)
VMF-533 Cherry Pt. F2H-4 (18)

31 JAN 1955

VC-3 Moffett F2H-3 (17)
Det A Essex F2H-3 (4)
Det C Kearsarge F2H-3 (8)
Det H Wasp F2H-3 (3)
VX-3 Atlantic City F2H-3 (2), F2H-4 (2)
VC-4 Atlantic City F2H-4 (13)
Det 33 Intrepid F2H-4 (4)
Det 34 L. Champlain F2H-4 (5)
Det 35 Midway F2H-4 (4)
VF-11 Cecil F2H-4 (10)
VF-23 Moffett F2H-3 (13)
VF-31 Cecil F2H-3 (13)
VF-41 Randolph F2H-3 (12)
VF-71 Leeward Pt. F2H-3 (16)
VF-141 Miramar F2H-3 (14)
VF-152 Yorktown F2H-3 (11)
VF-171 Jacksonville F2H-3 (13)
VF-193 Moffett F2H-3 (11)
NAF Opama F2H-3 (1)
FASRONS:
2 Quonset Pt. F2H-3 (1)
4 North Island F2H-3 (1), F2H-4 (2)
11 Atsugi F2H-3 (3)
117 Barbers Pt. F2H-4 (2)

119 Sangley Pt. F2H-3 (1)
USMC
VMF-114 Cherry Pt. F2H-4 (14)
VMF-214 Kaneohe F2H-4 (23)
VMF-533 Cherry Pt. F2H-4 (24)

28 FEB 1955

VC-3 Moffett F2H-3 (18)
Det A Essex F2H-3 (4)
Det C Kearsarge F2H-3 (8)
Det H Wasp F2H-4 (3)
VC-4 Atlantic City F2H-4 (3)
Det 33 Intrepid F2H-4 (4)
Det 35 Midway F2H-4 (4)
Det 39 Ticonderoga F2H-4 (7)
VX-5 Moffett F2H-3 (2)
VF-11 Cecil F2H-4 (11)
VF-23 Moffett F2H-3 (11)
VF-31 Cecil F2H-3 (12)
VF-41 Randolph F2H-3 (11)
VF-71 Leeward Pt. F2H-3 (17)
VF-141 Miramar F2H-3 (14)
VF-152 Yorktown F2H-3 (9)
VF-171 Jacksonville F2H-3 (12)
VF-193 Oriskany F2H-3 (9)
NAMTC Point Mugu F2H-3 (1)
NAOTS Chincoteague F2H-3 (1)
NASWF Kirtland AFB F2H-3 (1)
NADU S. Weymouth F2H-4 (2)
FASRONS:
4 North Island F2H-4 (5)
8 Alameda F2H-4 (1)
104 Pt. Lyauty F2H-3 (1)
117 Barbers Pt. F2H-4 (2)
USMC
VMF-214 Kaneohe F2H-4 (23)
VMF-533 Cherry Pt. F2H-4 (24)

31 MAR 1955

VC-3 Moffett F2H-3 (18)
Det A Essex F2H-3 (4)
Det C Kearsarge F2H-3 (8)
Det H Wasp F2H-4 (3)
VX-3 Atlantic City F2H-4 (2)
VC-4 Atlantic City F2H-4 (18)
Det 34 L. Champlain F2H-4 (5)
Det 35 Midway F2H-4 (3)
Det 39 Ticonderoga F2H-4 (7)
VX-5 Moffett F2H-3 (2)
VF-11 Cecil F2H-4 (11)
VF-23 Moffett F2H-3 (10)
VF-31 Cecil F2H-3 (14)
VF-41 Randolph F2H-3 (11)
VF-71 Quonset Pt. F2H-3 (13)
VF-141 Miramar F2H-3 (14)
VF-152 Moffett F2H-3 (7)
VF-171 Coral Sea F2H-3 (12)
VF-193 Oriskany F2H-3 (9)
NAMTC Point Mugu F2H-3 (1)
NAOTS Chincoteague F2H-3 (1)
NASWF Kirtland AFB F2H-3 (1)
NADU S. Weymouth F2H-4 (2)
FASRONS:
2 Quonset Pt F2H-3 (1)
4 North Island F2H-3 (2)
6 Jacksonville F2H-3 (2)
11 Atsugi F2H-3 (2), F2H-4 (2)
14 Miramar F2H-3 (6)
104 Pt. Lyauty F2H-3 (1)
117 Barbers Pt. F2H-4 (3)
119 Sangley Pt. F2H-3 (3)
USMC
VMF-214 Kaneohe F2H-4 (24)
VMF-533 Cherry Pt. F2H-4 (24)

30 APR 1955

Unit	Location	Aircraft
VC-3	Moffett	F2H-3 (20)
Det A	Essex	F2H-3 (4)
Det C	Kearsarge	F2H-3 (7)
VX-3	Atlantic City	F2H-3 (2), F2H-4 (2)
VC-4	Atlantic City	F2H-4 (27)
Det 33	Intrepid	F2H-4 (6)
Det 35	Midway	F2H-4 (4)
VX-5	Moffett	F2H-3 (2)
VF-11	Cecil	F2H-4 (12)
VF-23	Moffett	F2H-3 (10)
VF-31	Coral Sea	F2H-3 (15)
VF-41	Randolph	F2H-3 (11), F2H-4 (1)
VF-71	Quonset Pt.	F2H-3 (11)
VF-82	Oceana	F2H-4 (3), F2H-2 (2), F2H-2B (1), F2H-2N (4)
VF-141	Miramar	F2H-3 (14)
VF-152	Moffett	F2H-3 (9)
VF-171	Coral Sea	F2H-3 (12)
VF-193	Oriskany	F2H-3 (9)
NAMTC	Point Mugu	F2H-3 (1)
NAOTS	Chincoteague	F2H-3 (1)
NASWF	Kirtland AFB	F2H-3 (1)
NADU	S. Weymouth	F2H-4 (2)

FASRONS:

2	Quonset Pt	F2H-3 (1)
3	Norfolk	F2H-3 (1)
4	North Island	F2H-3 (4)
6	Jacksonville	F2H-3 (1)
10	Moffett	F2H-3 (9)
11	Atsugi	F2H-3 (3)
117	Barbers Pt.	F2H-4 (1)

USMC

VMF-214	Kaneohe	F2H-4 (23)
VMF-533	Cherry Pt.	F2H-4 (24)

31 MAY 1955

Unit	Location	Aircraft
VC-3	Moffett	F2H-3 (17)
Det A	Essex	F2H-3 (3)
VX-3	Atlantic City	F2H-3 (2), F2H-4 (3)
VC-4	Atlantic City	F2H-4 (19)
Det 30	Bennington	F2H-4 (8)
Det 33	Intrepid	F2H-4 (4)
Det 35	Midway	F2H-4 (4)
VX-5	Moffett	F2H-3 (2)
VF-11	Cecil	F2H-4 (12)
VF-23	Moffett	F2H-3 (10)
VF-31	Key West	F2H-3 (13)
VF-41	Randolph	F2H-3 (11), F2H-4 (1)
VF-71	Leeward Pt.	F2H-3 (11)
VF-82	Oceana	F2H-4 (6), F2H-2 (2), F2H-2B (1), F2H-2N (1)
VF-141	Miramar	F2H-3 (15)
VF-152	Moffett	F2H-3 (9)
VF-171	Coral Sea	F2H-3 (12)
VF-193	Oriskany	F2H-3 (9)
NAMTC	Point Mugu	F2H-3 (1)
NAOTS	Chincoteague	F2H-3 (1)
NASWF	Kirtland AFB	F2H-3 (1)
NADU	S. Weymouth	F2H-4 (2)
NAF	Oppama	F2H-4 (1)

FASRONS:

2	Quonset Pt	F2H-3 (1)
6	Jacksonville	F2H-3 (3)
104	Pt. Lyautey	F2H-4 (1)
117	Barbers Pt.	F2H-4 (1)
119	Sangley Pt.	F2H-3 (1)

USMC

VMF-214	Kaneohe	F2H-4 (23)
VMF-533	Cherry Pt.	F2H-4 (24)

30 JUN 1955

Unit	Location	Aircraft
VC-3	Moffett	F2H-3 (17)
VC-4	Atlantic City	F2H-4 (17)
Det 30	Bennington	F2H-4 (5)
Det 33	Intrepid	F2H-4 (4)
Det 35	Midway	F2H-4 (4)
VX-5	Moffett	F2H-3 (2)
VF-11	Key West	F2H-4 (13)
VF-23	Moffett	F2H-3 (9)
VF-31	Cecil	F2H-3 (13)
VF-41	Oceana	F2H-3 (12), F2H-4 (1)
VF-52	Alameda	F2H-3 (5)
VF-71	Hornet	F2H-3 (11)
VF-82	Oceana	F2H-4 (14)
VF-114	Miramar	F2H-3 (6)
VF-141	Miramar	F2H-3 (14)
VF-152	Moffett	F2H-3 (9)
VF-171	Coral Sea	F2H-3 (11)
VF-193	Oriskany	F2H-3 (8)
VF-194	Moffett	F2H-3 (7)
NAMTC	Point Mugu	F2H-3 (1)
NAOTS	Chincoteague	F2H-3 (1)
NASWF	Kirtland AFB	F2H-3 (1)
NADU	S. Weymouth	F2H-4 (2)
BAR R&D	Baltimore	F2H-3 (2)
R&D	St. Louis	F2H-3 (2)
NAF	Oppama	F2H-4 (1)
NACA	Langley	F2H-3 (1)
INN	Boston	F2H-3M (1)
INN	Minneapolis	F2H-3 (1)

FASRONS:

4	North Island	F2H-3 (3)
8	Alameda	F2H-4 (1)
10	Moffett	F2H-3 (11)
11	Atsugi	F2H-3 (4)
12	Miramar	F2H-3 (3)
104	Pt. Lyautey	F2H-4 (1)
117	Barbers Pt.	F2H-4 (1)
119	Sangley Pt.	F2H-3 (1)

USMC:

VMF-214	Kaneohe	F2H-4 (20)
VMF-533	Cherry Pt.	F2H-4 (18)

31 JULY 1955

Unit	Location	Aircraft
VC-3	Moffett	F2H-3 (13)
VX-3	Atlantic City	F2H-3 (1), F2H-4 (3)
VC-4	Atlantic City	F2H-4 (21)
Det 30	Bennington	F2H-4 (1)
Det 33	Intrepid	F2H-4 (4)
VX-5	Moffett	F2H-3 (1)
VF-11	Cecil	F2H-4 (12)
VF-23	Moffett	F2H-3 (9)
VF-31	Cecil	F2H-3 (13)
VF-41	Oceana	F2H-3 (10)
VF-52	Alameda	F2H-3 (7)
VF-71	Hornet	F2H-3 (11)
VF-82	Oceana	F2H-4 (14)
VF-102	Bennington	F2H-4 (5)
VF-114	Miramar	F2H-3 (7)
VF-141	Miramar	F2H-3 (12)
VF-152	Moffitt	F2H-3 (9)
VF-171	Coral Sea	F2H-3 (11)
VF-193	Oriskany	F2H-3 (8)
VF-213	Moffett	F2H-3 (4)
NASWF	Kirtland AFB	F2H-3 (1)
NACA	Langley	F2H-3 (1)
NADU		F2H-4 (2)
NAMTC	Point Mugu	F2H-3M (1)
NAOTS	Chin	F2H-4 (1)
NOTS	Inyokern	F2H-3 (3)

FASRONS:

4	North Island	F2H-3 (2)
6	Jacksonville	F2H-3 (1)
8	Alameda	F2H-4 (3)
10	Moffett	F2H-3 (2)

USMC

VMF-214	Kaneohe	F2H-4 (14)

31 AUG 1955

Unit	Location	Aircraft
VMF-533	Cherry Pt.	F2H-4 (18)
VC-3	Moffett	F2H-3 (6)
Det G	Hancock	F2H-3 (4)
VX-3	Atlantic City	F2H-3 (1), F2H-4 (3)
VC-4	Atlantic City	F2H-4 (9)
Det 30	Bennington	F2H-4 (5)
Det 33	Intrepid	F2H-4 (3)
Det 34	L. Champlain	F2H-4 (4)
VX-5	Moffett	F2H-3 (1)
VF-11	Cecil	F2H-4 (11)
VF-23	Moffett	F2H-3 (10)
VF-31	Cecil	F2H-3 (14)
VF-41	Oceana	F2H-3 (10)
VF-52	Alameda	F2H-3 (8)
VF-71	Hornet	F2H-3 (12)
VF-82	Oceana	F2H-4 (12)
VF-102	Bennington	F2H-4 (5)
VF-114	Miramar	F2H-3 (8)
VF-141	Miramar	F2H-3 (12)
VF-152	Moffitt	F2H-3 (9)
VF-171	Coral Sea	F2H-3 (11)
VF-193	Oriskany	F2H-3 (6)
VF-194	Moffett	F2H-3 (8)
VF-213	Moffett	F2H-3 (7)
NASWF	Kirtland AFB	F2H-3 (1)
NACA	Langley	F2H-3 (1)
NADU		F2H-4 (2)
NAMTC	Point Mugu	F2H-3M (1)
NAOTS	Chin	F2H-4 (1)
NOTS	Inyokern	F2H-3 (3)

FASRONS:

4	North Island	F2H-3 (4)
8	Alameda	F2H-4 (1)
117	Barbers Pt.	F2H-4 (2)

USMC

VMF-214	Kaneohe	F2H-4 (14)
VMF-533	Cherry Pt.	F2H-4 (18)

30 SEP 1955

Unit	Location	Aircraft
VC-3	Moffett	F2H-3 (6)
Det G	Hancock	F2H-3 (4)
VX-3	Atlantic City	F2H-3 (1), F2H-4 (3)
VC-4	Atlantic City	F2H-4 (9)
Det 30	Bennington	F2H-4 (2)
Det 33	Intrepid	F2H-4 (2)
Det 34	L. Champlain	F2H-4 (5)
VX-5	Moffett	F2H-3 (1)
VF-11	Cecil	F2H-4 (12)
VF-23	Moffett	F2H-3 (9)
VF-31	Cecil	F2H-3 (15)
VF-41	Oceana	F2H-3 (11)
VF-52	Alameda	F2H-3 (8)
VF-64	Alameda	F2H-3 (8), F9F-5 (3)
VF-71	Hornet	F2H-3 (12)
VF-82	Oceana	F2H-3 (12)
VF-102	Bennington	F2H-4 (6)
VF-114	Miramar	F2H-3 (8)
VF-141	Miramar	F2H-3 (11)
VF-152	Moffitt	F2H-3 (8)
VF-171	Coral Sea	F2H-3 (11)
VF-193	Moffett	F2H-3 (6)
VF-194	Moffett	F2H-3 (8)
VF-213	Moffett	F2H-3 (8)
NASWF	Kirtland AFB	F2H-3 (1)
NACA	Langley	F2H-3 (1)
NADU		F2H-4 (1)
NAMTC	Point Mugu	F2H-3M (1)
NOTS	Inyokern	F2H-3 (3)

USMC

VMF-214	Kaneohe	F2H-4 (14)
VMF-533	Cherry Pt.	F2H-4 (17)

31 OCT 1955

VC-3	Moffett	F2H-3 (6)
Det G	Hancock	F2H-3 (4)
VX-3	Atlantic City	F2H-3 (1), F2H-4 (3)
VC-4	Atlantic City	F2H-4 (9)
Det 30	Bennington	F2H-4 (2)
Det 33	Intrepid	F2H-4 (2)
Det 34	L. Champlain	F2H-4 (5)
VX-5	Moffett	F2H-3 (1)
VF-11	Cecil	F2H-4 (10)
VF-23	Moffett	F2H-3 (10)
VF-31	Ticonderoga	F2H-3 (12)
VF-41	Oceana	F2H-3 (11)
VF-52	Alameda	F2H-3 (8)
VF-64	Alameda	F2H-3 (8)
VF-71	Hornet	F2H-3 (12)
VF-82	Key West	F2H-4 (12)
VF-102	Bennington	F2H-4 (8), F3D-2 (1)
VF-114	Miramar	F2H-3 (7)
VF-141	Kearsarge	F2H-3 (10)
VF-152	Moffitt	F2H-3 (7)
VF-171	Jacksonville	F2H-3 (14)
VF-193	Moffett	F2H-3 (6)
VF-194	Oriskany	F2H-3 (8)
VF-213	Moffett	F2H-3 (7)
NASWF	Kirtland AFB	F2H-3 (1)
NACA	Langley	F2H-3 (1)
NAMTC	Point Mugu	F2H-3M (1)
FASRONS:		
6	Jacksonville	F2H-3 (1)
9	Cecil	F2H-3 (1)
USMC		
VMF-214	Kaneohe	F2H-4 (10), F9F-6 (1)
VMF-533	Cherry Pt.	F2H-4 (16)

30 NOV 1955

VC-3	Moffett	F2H-3 (5)
Det G	Hancock	F2H-3 (4)
VX-3	Atlantic City	F2H-3 (1), F2H-4 (3)
VC-4	Atlantic City	F2H-4 (9)
Det 30	Bennington	F2H-4 (4)
Det 34	L. Champlain	F2H-4 (4)
VX-5	Moffett	F2H-3 (1)
VF-11	Cecil	F2H-4 (14)
VF-23	Moffett	F2H-3 (10)
VF-31	Ticonderoga	F2H-3 (11)
VF-41	Oceana	F2H-3 (9)
VF-52	Alameda	F2H-3 (8)
VF-64	Alameda	F2H-3 (7)
VF-71	Hornet	F2H-3 (12)
VF-82	Oceana	F2H-4 (12)
VF-102	Bennington	F2H-4 (10), F3D-2 (1)
VF-114	Miramar	F2H-3 (7)
VF-141	Kearsarge	F2H-3 (10)
VF-152	Moffitt	F2H-3 (7)
VF-171	Jacksonville	F2H-3 (11)
VF-193	Moffett	F2H-3 (6)
VF-194	Oriskany	F2H-3 (8)
VF-213	Moffett	F2H-3 (7)
NASWF	Kirtland AFB	F2H-3 (1)
NACA	Langley	F2H-3 (1)
NAMTC	Point Mugu	F2H-3M (1)
FASRONS:		
2	Quonset Pt.	F2H-3 (2)
4	North Island	F2H-3 (1)
9	Cecil	F2H-3 (1)
10	Moffett	F2H-3 (1)
104	Pt. Lyauty	F2H-4 (1)
117	Barbers Pt.	F2H-4 (2)
USMC		
VMF-214	Kaneohe	F2H-4 (10), F9F-6 (1)
VMF-533	Cherry Pt.	F2H-4 (15)

31 DEC 1955

VC-3	Moffett	F2H-3 (1)

Det G	Hancock	F2H-3 (4)
Det J	Moffett	F2H-3 (4)
VX-3	Atlantic City	F2H-3 (1), F2H-4 (3)
VC-4	Atlantic City	F2H-4 (7)
Det 30	Bennington	F2H-4 (3)
Det 34	L. Champlain	F2H-4 (4)
VX-5	Moffett	F2H-3 (1)
VF-11	Cecil	F2H-4 (6)
VF-23	Moffett	F2H-3 (9)
VF-31	Ticonderoga	F2H-3 (11)
VF-41	Oceana	F2H-3 (9)
VF-52	Alameda	F2H-3 (6)
VF-64	Alameda	F2H-3 (7)
VF-71	Hornet	F2H-3 (12)
VF-82	Oceana	F2H-4 (12)
VF-102	Key West	F2H-4 (12), F3D-2 (1)
VF-114	Miramar	F2H-3 (7)
VF-141	Kearsarge	F2H-3 (9)
VF-152	Moffitt	F2H-3 (8)
VF-171	Jacksonville	F2H-3 (10)
VF-193	Moffett	F2H-3 (5)
VF-194	Oriskany	F2H-3 (8)
VF-213	Moffett	F2H-3 (6)
NASWF	Kirtland AFB	F2H-3 (1)
NACA	Langley	F2H-3 (1)
NAMTC	Point Mugu	F2H-3M (1)
FASRONS:		
2	Quonset Pt.	F2H-3 (1)
4	North Island	F2H-3 (2)
8	Alameda	F2H-4 (4)
10	Moffett	F2H-3 (4)
104	Pt. Lyauty	F2H-4 (1)
119	Sangley Pt.	F2H-3 (2)
USMC:		
VMF-214	Kaneohe	F2H-4 (12), F9F-8 (1)
VMF-533	Cherry Pt.	F2H-4 (19)

31 JAN 1956

VC-3	Moffett	F2H-3 (2)
Det G	Hancock	F2H-3 (4)
Det J	Shangri-La	F2H-3 (4)
VC-4	Atlantic City	
VF-11	Cecil	F2H-4 (14)
VF-23	Moffett	F2H-3 (9)
VF-31	Ticonderoga	F2H-3 (9)
VF-41	Forrestal	F2H-3 (11)
VF-52	Alameda	F2H-3 (8)
VF-64	Alameda	F2H-3 (8)
VF-71	Hornet	F2H-3 (10)
VF-82	Oceana	F2H-4 (12)
VF-102	Key West	F2H-4 (12), F3D-2 (1)
VF-114	Miramar	F2H-3 (8)
VF-141	Kearsarge	F2H-3 (9)
VF-152	Moffitt	F2H-3 (7)
VF-171	Jacksonville	F2H-3 (11)
VF-172	Jacksonville	F2H-4 (1), F2H-2 (12)
VF-193	Moffett	F2H-3 (7)
VF-194	Oriskany	F2H-3 (8)
VF-213	Moffett	F2H-3 (7)
NASWF	Kirtland AFB	F2H-3 (1)
NACA	Langley	F2H-3 (1)
NAMTC	Point Mugu	F2H-3M (1)
FASRONS:		
2	Quonset Pt.	F2H-3 (1)
119	Sangley Pt.	F2H-3 (2)
USMC:		
VMF(AW)-214	Kaneohe	F2H-4 (12), F9F-8 (1)
VMF(AW)-533	Chy Pt.	F2H-4 (19)

28 FEB 1956

VC-3	Moffett	
Det G	Hancock	F2H-3 (4)
Det J	Shangri-La	F2H-3 (3)
VC-4	Atlantic City	F2H-4 (5)

Det 30	Bennington	F2H-4 (2)
VF-11	Cecil	F2H-4 (14)
VF-23	Moffett	F2H-3 (9)
VF-31	Ticonderoga	F2H-3 (9)
VF-41	Forrestal	F2H-3 (11)
VF-52	Alameda	F2H-3 (8)
VF-64	Alameda	F2H-3 (8)
VF-71	Quonset Pt.	F2H-3 (11)
VF-82	Intrepid	F2H-4 (12)
VF-102	Ceciil	F2H-4 (13), F3D-2 (1)
VF-114	Miramar	F2H-3 (8)
VF-141	Kearsarge	F2H-3 (9)
VF-152	Moffitt	F2H-3 (9)
VF-171	Jacksonville	F2H-3 (10)
VF-172	Jacksonville	F2H-4 (1), F2H-2 (12)
VF-193	Moffett	F2H-3 (8)
VF-194	Oriskany	F2H-3 (8)
VF-213	Moffett	F2H-3 (8)
NASWF	Kirtland AFB	F2H-3 (1)
NACA	Langley	F2H-3 (1)
NAMTC	Point Mugu	F2H-3M (1)
FASRONS:		
8	Alameda	F2H-3 (1), F2H-4 (6)
10	Moffett	F2H-3 (4)
11	Atsugi	F2H-3 (4)
104	Pt. Lyautry	F2H-4 (1)
USMC:		
VMF-214	Kaneohe	F2H-4 (12), F9F-8 (1)
VMF-533	Rosevelt Rds,	F2H-4 (19)

31 MAR 1956

VC-3	Moffett	
Det J	Shangri-La	F2H-3 (4)
VC-4	Atlantic City	
Det 30	Bennington	F2H-4 (2)
VF-11	Coral Sea	F2H-4 (11)
VF-22	Jacksonville	F2H-4 (13), F2H-2 (1)
VF-23	Yorktown	F2H-3 (10)
VF-31	Ticonderoga	F2H-3 (8)
VF-41	Jacksonville	F2H-3 (9)
VF-52	Alameda	F2H-3 (8)
VF-64	Alameda	F2H-3 (8)
VF-71	Quonset Pt.	F2H-3 (11)
VF-82	Intrepid	F2H-4 (12)
VF-102	Randolph	F2H-4 (12), F3D-2 (1)
VF-114	Miramar	F2H-3 (8)
VF-141	Kearsarge	F2H-3 (7)
VF-152	Moffitt	F2H-3 (10)
VF-171	Jacksonville	F2H-3 (11)
VF-193	Moffett	F2H-3 (8)
VF-194	Oriskany	F2H-3 (8)
VF-213	Moffett	F2H-3 (8)
NACA	Langley	F2H-3 (1)
NAMTC	Point Mugu	F2H-3M (1)
FASRONS:		
6	Jacksonville	F2H-4 (3)
104	Pt. Lyauty	F2H-4 (1)
USMC:		
VMF-214	Kaneohe	F2H-4 (14), F9F-8 (1)
VMF-533	Cherry Pt.	F2H-3 (1), F2H-4 (18)

30 APR 1956

VC-3	Moffett	
Det J	Shangri-La	F2H-3 (3)
VC-4	Atlantic City	F2H-4 (4)
VF-11	Cecil	F2H-4 (12)
VF-22	Jacksonville	F2H-4 (13), F2H-2 (1)
VF-23	Yorktown	F2H-3 (9)
VF-31	Ticonderoga	F2H-3 (8)
VF-41	Oceana	F2H-3 (11)
VF-52	Alameda	F2H-3 (8)
VF-64	Alameda	F2H-3 (8)
VF-71	Quonset Pt.	F2H-3 (12), TV-2 (2)
VF-82	Intrepid	F2H-4 (11)
VF-102	Randolph	F2H-4 (12)

VF-114 Miramar F2H-3 (8)
VF-141 Kearsarge F2H-3 (6)
VF-152 Wasp F2H-3 (8)
VF-171 Jacksonville F2H-3 (11)
VF-193 Moffett F2H-3 (9)
VF-194 Oriskany F2H-3 (8)
VF-213 Moffett F2H-3 (10)
NACA Langley F2H-3 (1)
NAMTC Point Mugu F2H-3M (1)
FASRONS:
4 North Island F2H-3 (2)
8 Alameda F2H-4 (1)
12 Miramar F2H-4 (1)
104 Pt. Lyauty F2H-4 (1)
USMC:
VMF-214 Kaneohe F2H-4 (19)
VMF-533 Cherry Pt. F2H-3 (1), F2H-4 (20)

31 MAY 1956
VF-11 Cecil F2H-4 (12)
VF-22 Jacksonville F2H-4 (12), F2H-2 (1)
VF-23 Yorktown F2H-3 (9)
VF-31 Ticonderoga F2H-3 (8)
VF-41 Oceana F2H-3 (11)
VF-52 Lexington F2H-3 (8)
VF-64 Alameda F2H-3 (8)
VF-71 Quonset Pt. F2H-3 (9), TV-2 (2)
VF-82 Intrepid F2H-4 (11)
VF-102 Randolph F2H-4 (14)
VF-114 Miramar F2H-3 (9)
VF-141 Miramar F2H-3 (6)
VF-152 Wasp F2H-3 (8)
VF-171 Jacksonville F2H-3 (11)
VF-193 Moffett F2H-3 (10)
VF-194 Oriskany F2H-3 (8)
VF-213 Moffett F2H-3 (9)
NACA Langley F2H-3 (1)
NAMTC Point Mugu F2H-3M (1)
FASRONS:
10 Moffett F2H-3 (3)
11 Atsugi F2H-3 (1)
12 Miramar F2H-3 (2)
USMC:
VMF-214 Kaneohe F2H-4 (20), F9F-8B (1)
VMF-533 Cherry Pt. F2H-3 (2), F2H-4 (18)

30 JUN 1956
VFAW-4 Antietam F2H-4 (5)
VF-11 Cecil F2H-4 (12)
VF-22 Jacksonville F2H-3 (1), F2H-4 (12)
VF-23 Yorktown F2H-3 (10)
VF-31 Ticonderoga F2H-3 (8), F2H-4 (1)
VF-41 Oceana F2H-3 (11)
VF-52 Lexington F2H-3 (8)
VF-64 Alameda F2H-3 (8)
VF-71 Quonset Pt. F2H-3 (1), F2H-4 (9)
VF-82 Intrepid F2H-4 (10)
VF-102 Randolph F2H-4 (14)
VF-114 Miramar F2H-3 (10)
VF-122 Miramar F2H-3 (1)
VF-141 Miramar F2H-3 (5)
VF-152 Wasp F2H-3 (8)
VF-171 F.D.R. F2H-3 (10)
VF-193 Moffett F2H-3 (10)
VF-194 Oriskany F2H-3 (8)
VF-213 Moffett F2H-3 (8)
NAMTC Point Mugu F2H-3M (1)
NAS North Island F2H-4 (2)
FASRONS:
4 North Island F2H-3 (1)
11 Atsugi F2H-3 (6)
12 Miramar F2H-3 (1)
104 Pt. Lyautey F2H-4 (1)
117 Barbers Pt. F2H-4 (1)
119 Sangley Pt. F2H-3 (1)

USMC:
VMF-214 Kaneohe F2H-4 (19)
VMF-533 Cherry Pt. F2H-4 (24)

31 JUL 1956
VFAW-4 Atlantic City F2H-4 (1)
VF-11 Cecil F2H-4 (12)
VF-22 Jacksonville F2H-4 (12)
VF-23 Yorktown F2H-3 (9)
VF-31 Ticonderoga F2H-3 (9)
VF-41 Oceana F2H-3 (13)
VF-52 Lexington F2H-3 (8)
VF-64 Alameda F2H-3 (8)
VF-71 Quonset Pt F2H-3 (10), TV-2 (2)
VF-82 Intrepid F2H-4 (12)
VF-102 Randolph F2H-4 (12)
VF-114 Essex F2H-3 (8)
VF-122 Miramar F2H-3 (3), F9F-8B (5)
VF-152 Wasp F2H-3 (7)
VF-171 Jacksonville F2H-3 (11)
VF-193 Moffett F2H-3 (10)
VF-194 Oriskany F2H-3 (8)
VF-213 Moffett F2H-3 (8)
NACA Langley F2H-3 (1)
NAMTC Point Mugu F2H-3M (2)
FASRONS:
4 North Island F2H-3 (2)
8 Alameda F2H-4 (2)
10 Moffett F2H-3 (2)
USMC:
VMF-214 Kaneohe F2H-4 (19), F9F-8B (1)
VMF-533 Ch. Pt. F2H-3 (1), F2H-4 (3)

31 AUG 1956
VF-11 Coral Sea F2H-4 (12)
VF-22 Saratoga F2H-4 (11)
VF-23 Moffett F2H-3 (5)
VF-31 Cecil F2H-3 (6)
VF-41 Oceana F2H-3 (13)
VF-52 Lexington F2H-3 (7)
VF-64 Alameda F2H-3 (8)
VF-71 Quonset Pt F2H-3 (10), TV-2 (2)
VF-82 Oceana F2H-4 (10)
VF-102 Coral Sea F2H-4 (12)
VF-114 Essex F2H-3 (8)
VF-122 Miramar F2H-3 (5)
VF-152 Wasp F2H-3 (8)
VF-171 F.D.R F2H-3 (10)
VF-193 Moffett F2H-3 (9)
VF-194 Alameda F2H-3 (8)
VF-213 B.H. Richard F2H-3 (8)
NACA Langley F2H-3 (1)
NAMTC Point Mugu F2H-3M (2)
USMC:
VMF-214 Kaneohe F2H-4 (21), F9F-8B (1)
VMF-533 Ch. Pt. F2H-4 (21)

30 SEP 1956
VF-11 Coral Sea F2H-4 (12)
VF-22 Saratoga F2H-4 (11)
VF-23 Moffett F2H-3 (5)
VF-31 Cecil F2H-3 (4)
VF-41 Oceana F2H-3 (13)
VF-52 Lexington F2H-3 (7)
VF-64 Alameda F2H-3 (8)
VF-71 Quonset Pt F2H-3 (8), TV-2 (2)
VF-82 Oceana F2H-4 (10)
VF-102 Randolph F2H-4 (12)
VF-114 Essex F2H-3 (8)
VF-122 Miramar F2H-3 (6)
VF-152 Wasp F2H-3 (8)
VF-171 F.D.R F2H-3 (10)
VF-193 Moffett F2H-3 (9)
VF-194 Alameda F2H-3 (6)
VF-213 B.H. Richard F2H-3 (8)

NACA Langley F2H-3 (1)
NAMTC Point Mugu F2H-3M (2)
FASRONS:
4 North Island F2H-3 (3)
8 Alameda F2H-3 (1)
10 Moffett F2H-3 (6)
11 Atsugi F2H-3 (1)
USMC:
VMF-214 Kaneohe F2H-4 (21), F9F-8B (1)
VMF-533 Ch. Pt. F2H-4 (21)

31 OCT 1956
VF-11 Coral Sea F2H-4 (14)
VF-22 Oceana F2H-4 (10)
VF-23 Moffett F2H-3 (3)
VF-31 Cecil F2H-3 (2)
VF-41 Bennington F2H-3 (11)
VF-52 Lexington F2H-3 (7)
VF-64 Shangri-La F2H-3 (8)
VF-71 Quonset Pt F2H-3 (8), TV-2 (2)
VF-82 Oceana F2H-4 (10)
VF-92 Alameda F2H-3 (1), F9F-5 (7)
VF-102 Randolph F2H-4 (12)
VF-114 Essex F2H-3 (8)
VF-122 Miramar F2H-3 (6)
VF-152 Wasp F2H-3 (7)
VF-171 F.D.R F2H-3 (10)
VF-193 Moffett F2H-3 (9)
VF-194 Alameda F2H-3 (9)
VF-213 B.H. Richard F2H-3 (8)
NACA Langley F2H-3 (1)
NAMTC Point Mugu F2H-3M (2)
FASRONS:
4 North Island F2H-3 (1)
8 Alameda F2H-3 (1), F2H-4 (1)
11 Atsugi F2H-3 (5)
USMC:
VMF-214 Kaneohe F2H-4 (20), F9F-8 (1)
VMF-533 Ch. Pt. F2H-4 (19)

30 NOV 1956
VF-11 Coral Sea F2H-4 (13)
VF-22 Oceana F2H-3 (2), F2H-4 (10)
VF-23 Moffett F2H-3 (3)
VF-31 Cecil F2H-3 (1), F3H-2N (9)
VF-41 Bennington F2H-3 (12)
VF-52 Lexington F2H-3 (7)
VF-64 Shangri-La F2H-3 (6)
VF-71 Quonset Pt F2H-3 (7), TV-2 (2)
VF-82 Oceana F2H-3 (2), F2H-4 (3)
VF-92 Alameda F2H-3 (9), F9F-5 (6)
VF-102 Randolph F2H-4 (12)
VF-114 Essex F2H-3 (8)
VF-122 Miramar F2H-3 (3)
VF-152 Moffett F2H-3 (7)
VF-171 Forrestal F2H-3 (5), F2H-4 (5)
VF-193 Moffett F2H-3 (8)
VF-194 Alameda F2H-3 (9)
VF-213 B.H. Richard F2H-3 (7)
NACA Langley F2H-3 (1)
NAMTC Point Mugu F2H-3M (2)
FASRONS:
4 North Island F2H-3 (2)
8 Alameda F2H-4 (1)
10 Moffett F2H-3 (1)
11 Atsugi F2H-3 (4)
USMC:
VMF-214 Kaneohe F2H-4 (19), F9F-8B (1)
VMF-533 Cherry Pt. F2H-4 (18)

31 DEC 1956
VF-11 Coral Sea F2H-4 (11)
VF-22 Jacksonville F2H-3 (1), F2H-4 (11)
VF-23 Moffett F2H-3 (3)
VF-41 Bennington F2H-3 (12)

Unit	Location	Aircraft
VF-52	Lexington	F2H-3 (7)
VF-64	Shangri-La	F2H-3 (6)
VF-71	Quonset Pt	F2H-3 (7), TV-2 (2)
VF-82	Oceana	F2H-3 (2), F2H-4 (8)
VF-92	Alameda	F2H-3 (9), F9F-5 (3)
VF-102	Randolph	F2H-4 (11)
VF-114	Essex	F2H-3 (8)
VF-152	Moffett	F2H-3 (7)
VF-171	Jacksonville	F2H-3 (4), F2H-4 (5)
VF-193	Moffett	F2H-3 (8)
VF-194	Alameda	F2H-3 (11)
VF-213	B.H. Richard	F2H-3 (7)
NACA	Langley	F2H-3 (1)
NAMTC	Point Mugu	F2H-3M (2)
USMC:		
VMF-214	Hancock	F2H-4 (20), F9F-8B (1)
VMF-533	Ch. Pt.	F2H-4 (19)

31 JAN 1957

Unit	Location	Aircraft
VF-11	Coral Sea	F2H-4 (11)
VF-22	Jacksonville	F2H-4 (13)
VF-23	Moffett	F2H-4 (2), F4D-1 (3)
VF-41	Bennington	F2H-3 (12)
VF-52	Alameda	F2H-3 (7)
VF-64	Shangri-La	F2H-3 (9)
VF-71	Quonset Pt	F2H-3 (7)
VF-82	Oceana	F2H-4 (3), F3H-2N (9)
VF-92	Alameda	F2H-3 (9), F9F-5 (3)
VF-102	Randolph	F2H-4 (11)
VF-114	Miramar	F2H-3 (7)
VF-152	Moffett	F2H-3 (9)
VF-171	Jacksonville	F2H-3 (5), F2H-4 (1)
VF-193	Yorktown	F2H-3 (8)
VF-194	Alameda	F2H-3 (13)
VF-213	B.H. Richard	F2H-3 (10)
NACA	Langley	F2H-3 (1)
NAMTC	Point Mugu	F2H-3M (1)
USMC:		
VMF(AW)-214	Hancock	F2H-4 (20)
VMA(AW)-533	Ch. Pt.	F2H-4 (13)

31 MAR 1957

Unit	Location	Aircraft
VF-11	Cecil	F2H-4 (11)
VF-22	F.D.R.	F2H-4 (13)
VF-23	Moffett	F2H-3 (2)
VF-41	Bennington	F2H-3 (12)
VF-52	Alameda	F2H-3 (9)
VF-64	Shangri-La	F2H-3 (7)
VF-71	Quonset Pt	F2H-3 (9), F2H-4 (1)
VF-82	Oceana	F2H-4 (1)
VF-92	Alameda	F2H-3 (13)
VF-102	Cecil	F2H-4 (9)
VF-114	Miramar	F2H-3 (1), F3H-2N (5)
VF-152	Moffett	F2H-3 (10)
VF-171	F.D.R.	F2H-3 (10), F2H-4 (6)
VF-193	Yorktown	F2H-3 (8)
VF-194	Alameda	F2H-3 (11)
VF-213	B.H. Richard	F2H-3 (4)
NASWF	Kirtland AFB	F2H-3 (1)
NACA	Langley	F2H-3 (1)
NAMTC	Point Mugu	F2H-3M (1)
FASRONS:		
104	Pt. Lyauty	F2H-4 (1)
USMC:		
VMF(AW)-214	Hancock	F2H-4 (19)
VMF-333	Miami	F2H-3 (1), FJ-3 (14)
VMA(AW)-533	Ch. Pt.	F2H-4 (12)

30 APR 1957

Unit	Location	Aircraft
VF-11	Cecil	F2H-4 (10)
VF-22	Jacksonville	F2H-4 (13)
VF-41	Oceana	F2H-3 (12)
VF-52	Alameda	F2H-3 (11)
VF-64	Shangri-La	F2H-3 (7)
VF-71	Key West	F2H-3 (9), F2H-4 (1)

Unit	Location	Aircraft
VF-92	Alameda	F2H-3 (12)
VF-102	Cecil	F2H-4 (4)
VF-152	Moffett	F2H-3 (10)
VF-171	Jacksonville	F2H-3 (12), F2H-4 (5)
VF-193	Yorktown	F2H-3 (8)
VF-194	Alameda	F2H-3 (13)
VF-213	B.H. Richard	F2H-3 (4)
NASWF	Kirtland AFB	F2H-3 (1)
NACA	Langley	F2H-3 (1)
NAMTC	Point Mugu	F2H-3M (1)
FASRONS:		
8	Alameda	F2H-3 (1)
11	Atsugi	F2H-3 (5)
USMC:		
VMF(AW)-214	Hancock	F2H-4 (19)
VMF-333	Miami	F2H-3 (1), FJ-3 (22)
VMA(AW)-533	Ch. Pt.	F2H-4 (14)

31 MAY 1957

Unit	Location	Aircraft
VF-11	Cecil	F2H-4 (4)
VF-22	Jacksonville	F2H-4 (9)
VF-41	Oceana	F2H-3 (12)
VF-52	Alameda	F2H-3 (12)
VF-64	Alameda	F2H-3 (4)
VF-71	Intrepid	F2H-3 (8), F2H-4 (6)
VF-92	Alameda	F2H-3 (12)
VF-102	Cecil	F2H-4 (8), F4D-1 (9)
VF-152	Moffett	F2H-3 (12)
VF-171	Jacksonville	F2H-3 (12), F2H-4 (4)
VF-193	Yorktown	F2H-3 (8)
VF-194	Alameda	F2H-3 (13)
VF-213	Moffett	F2H-3 (8)
NASWF	Kirtland AFB	F2H-3 (1)
NACA	Langley	F2H-3 (1)
NAMTC	Point Mugu	F2H-3M (1)
FASRONS:		
117	Barbers Pt.	F2H-4 (2)
119	Sangley Pt.	F2H-3 (1)
USMC:		
VMF(AW)-214	Hancock	F2H-4 (16)
VMF-333	Miami	F2H-3 (1), FJ-3 (22)
VMA(AW)-533	Ch. Pt.	F2H-4 (14)

30 JUN 1957

Unit	Location	Aircraft
VFAW-4	Antietam	F2H-4 (5) ?
VF-11	Cecil	F2H-3 (1), F2H-4 (16)
VF-22	Jacksonville	F2H-4 (8)
VF-41	Oceana	F2H-3 (5)
VF-52	Alameda	F2H-3 (13)
VF-64	Alameda	F2H-3 (4)
VF-71	Intrepid	F2H-3 (7), F2H-4 (6)
VF-92	Alameda	F2H-3 (13)
VF-102	Cecil	F2H-4 (5)
VF-152	Moffett	F2H-3 (13)
VF-171	F.D.R.	F2H-3 (16)
VF-193	Yorktown	F2H-3 (8)
VF-194	Alameda	F2H-3 (12)
VF-213	Moffett	F2H-3 (8)
NAS	North Island	F2H-3 (1)
NAF	Oppama	F2H-3 (1)
NACA	Langley	F2H-3 (1)
NAMTC	Point Mugu	F2H-3M (1)
NART	NAS Oakland	F2H-3 (1)
FASRONS:		
117	Barbers Pt.	F2H-4 (2)
119	Sangley Pt.	F2H-3 (1)
USMC:		
VMF(AW)-214	Hancock	F2H-4 (16)
VMF-333	Miami	F2H-3 (1), FJ-3 (22)
VMA-533	Cherry Pt.	F2H-4 (12)

31 JUL 1957

Unit	Location	Aircraft
VF-11	Cecil	F2H-4 (14), F2H-3 (1)
VF-22	Randolph	F2H-4 (8)
VF-41	Oceana	F2H-3 (5), F3H-2M (8)
VF-52	Alameda	F2H-3 (12)

Unit	Location	Aircraft
VF-64	Alameda	F2H-3 (5)
VF-71	Intrepid	F2H-3 (7), F2H-4 (6)
VF-92	Alameda	F2H-3 (13)
VF-152	Moffett	F2H-3 (6)
VF-171	FDR	F2H-3 (20), F2H-3M (1)
VF-193	Yorktown	F2H-3 (8)
VF-194	Kearsarge	F2H-3 (10)
VF-213	B. H. Richard	F2H-3 (6)
NACA	Langley	F2H-3 (1)
NAMTC	Point Mugu	F2H-3M (1)
USMC:		
VMA-214	Hancock	F2H-4 (16)
VMF-333	Miami	F2H-4 (1), FJ-3 (22)
VMA-533	Cherry Pt	F2H-4 (14)

30 AUG 1957

Unit	Location	Aircraft
VF-11	Key West	F2H-4 (14), F2H-3 (1)
VF-22	Randolph	F2H-4 (8)
VF-41	Oceana	F2H-3 (3), F3H-2M (11)
VF-52	Alameda	F2H-3 (11)
VF-64	Shangri-La	F2H-3 (7)
VF-71	Intrepid	F2H-3 (5), F2H-4 (6)
VF-92	Alameda	F2H-3 (12)
VF-152	Moffett	F2H-3 (11)
VF-171	FDR	F2H-3 (13), F2H-3M (1)
VF-193	Moffett	F2H-3 (8)
VF-194	Kearsarge	F2H-3 (10)
NACA	Langley	F2H-3 (1)
NAMTC	Point Mugu	F2H-3M (1)
USMC:		
VMA-214	Hancock	F2H-4 (15)
VMF-333	Miami	F2H-4 (1), FJ-3 (22)
VMA-533	Cherry Pt	F2H-4 (14), F9F-8s (11)
FASRONS:		
2	Quonset Pt.	F2H-3 (1)
6	Jacksonville	F2H-3 (2)
11	Atsugi	F2H-3 (5)

30 SEP 1957

Unit	Location	Aircraft
VF-11	Key West	F2H-4 (16), F2H-3 (1)
VF-22	Randolph	F2H-4 (7)
VF-41	Oceana	F2H-3 (2), F3Hs (13)
VF-52	Alameda	F2H-3 (9)
VF-64	Alameda	F2H-3 (5), F3H-2M (4)
VF-71	Intrepid	F2H-3 (5), F2H-4 (6)
VF-92	Alameda	F2H-3 (12)
VF-152	Moffett	F2H-3 (12)
VF-171	FDR	F2H-3 (13), F2H-3M (1)
VF-193	Moffett	F2H-3 (6)
VF-194	Kearsarge	F2H-3 (8)
NACA	Langley	F2H-3 (1)
NAMTC	Point Mugu	F2H-3M (1)
USMC:		
VMA-214	Kaneohe	F2H-4 (15)
VMA-533	Cherry Pt	F2H-4 (11), F9F-8s (16)
FASRONS:		
2	Quoset Pt.	F2H-3 (1)
6	Jacksonville	F2H-3 (2)
11	Atsugi	F2H-3 (5)

31 OCT 1957

Unit	Location	Aircraft
VF-11	Cecil	F2H-4 (16), F2H-3 (1)
VF-22	Randolph	F2H-4 (8)
VF-41	Oceana	F2H-3 (1), F3Hs (15)
VF-52	Alameda	F2H-3 (9)
VF-64	Alameda	F2H-3 (2), F3Hs (4)
VF-71	Oceana	F2H-3 (5), F2H-4 (6)
VF-92	Alameda	F2H-3 (11)
VF-152	Moffett	F2H-3 (14)
VF-171	Oceana	F2H-3 (13)
VF-193	Moffett	F2H-3 (6)
VF-194	Kearsarge	F2H-3 (9)
NACA	Langley	F2H-3 (1)
NAMTC	Point Mugu	F2H-3M (1)

USMC:
VMA-214	Kaneohe	F2H-4 (13)
VMA-533	Cherry Pt	F2H-4 (4), F9F-8s (16)

FASRONS:
8	Alameda	F2H-4 (1)
11	Atsugi	F2H-3 (4)

30 NOV 1957
VFAW-4	Quonset Pt.	F2H-3 (3), F2H-4 (3)
VF-11	Cecil	F2H-4 (14), F2H-3 (1)
VF-22	Randolph	F2H-4 (8)
VF-52	Alameda	F2H-3 (9)
VF-64	Alameda	F2H-3 (12)
VF-71	Oceana	F2H-3 (5), F2H-4 (9)
VF-92	Alameda	F2H-3 (5)
VF-152	Moffett	F2H-3 (15)
VF-171	Oceana	F2H-3 (13), F2H-3M (1)
VF-193	Moffett	F2H-3 (2), F3H-2 (2)
VF-194	Kearsarge	F2H-3 (7)
NACA	Langley	F2H-3 (1)
NAMTC	Point Mugu	F2H-3M (1)

USMC:
VMA-214	Kaneohe	F2H-4 (13)
VMA-533	Cherry Pt	F2H-4 (4), F9F-8s (16)

FASRONS:
2	Quonset Pt.	F2H-3 (1)
8	Alameda	F2H-4 (4), F2H-3 (10)
11	Atsugi	F2H-3 (5)

31 DEC 1957
VFAW-4	Quonset Pt.	F2H-3 (7), F2H-4 (3)
VF-11	Cecil	F2H-4 (15), F2H-3 (1)
VF-22	Randolph	F2H-4 (8)
VF-52	Alameda	F2H-3 (12)
VF-64	Alameda	F2H-3 (10)
VF-71	Oceana	F2H-3 (5), F2H-4 (14)
VF-92	Alameda	F2H-3 (8)
VF-152	Hornet	F2H-3 (13)
VF-171	F.D.R.	F2H-3 (12)
VF-193	Moffett	F2H-3 (2)
VF-194	Kearsarge	F2H-3 (16)
NACA	Langley	F2H-3 (1)
NAMTC	Point Mugu	F2H-3M (1)

USMC:
VMA-214	Kaneohe	F2H-4 (5)
VMA-533	Cherry Pt	F2H-4 (1), F9F-8s (18)

FASRONS:
2	Quonset Pt.	F2H-3 (1)
8	Alameda	F2H-4 (3)
11	Atsugi	F2H-3 (3)
117	Barbers Pt	F2H-4 (9)

31 JAN 1958
VFAW-4	Quonset Pt.	F2H-3 (7), F2H-4 (7)
VF-11	Essex	F2H-4 (14)
VF-22	Randolph	F2H-4 (8)
VF-52	Alameda	F2H-3 (14)
VF-71	Oceana	F2H-3 (5), F2H-4 (14)
VF-92	Alameda	F2H-3 (17)
VF-152	Hornet	F2H-3 (10)
VF-171	F.D.R.	F2H-3 (12)
VF-194	Kearsarge	F2H-3 (9)
NAMTC	Point Mugu	F2H-3M (1)

USMC:
VMA-214	Kaneohe	F2H-4 (5), FJ-4 (1)

FASRONS:
8	Alameda	F2H-4 (3)
11	Atsugi	F2H-3 (1)

28 FEB 1958
VFAW-4	Quonset Pt.	F2H-3 (10), F2H-4 (7)
VF-11	Essex	F2H-4 (12)
VF-22	Randolph	F2H-4 (9)
VF-52	Alameda	F2H-3 (13)
VF-71	Oceana	F2H-3 (5), F2H-4 (16)
VF-92	Alameda	F2H-3 (21)
VF-152	Hornet	F2H-3 (10)
VF-171	F.D.R.	F2H-3 (12)
VF-194	Kearsarge	F2H-3 (9)
NAMTC	Point Mugu	F2H-3M (1)

USMC:
VMA-214	Kaneohe	F2H-4 (7), FJ-4 (1)

FASRONS:
6	Jacksonville	F2H-4 (2)
8	Alameda	F2H-4 (1)
9	Cecil	F2H-4 (1)
11	Atsugi	F2H-3 (1)

31 MAR 1958
VFAW-4	Quonset Pt.	F2H-3 (12), F2H-4 (13)
VF-11	Essex	F2H-4 (11)
VF-22	Jacksonville	F2H-3 (9), F2H-4 (8)
VF-52	Bennington	F2H-3 (14), F2H-4 (1)
VF-71	Oceana	F2H-4 (16)
VF-92	Alameda	F2H-3 (19)
VF-121	Miramar	F2H-4 (1)
VF-152	Hornet	F2H-3 (10)
VF-194	Kearsarge	F2H-3 (5)
NAMTC	Point Mugu	F2H-3M (1)

USMC:
VMA-214	Kaneohe	F2H-4 (5), FJ-4 (21)

FASRONS:
8	Alameda	F2H-4 (1)
11	Atsugi	F2H-3 (4)
117	Barbers Pt.	F2H-4 (2)
119	Sangley Pt	F2H-3 (1)

30 APR 1958
VFAW-4	Quonset Pt.	F2H-3 (9), F2H-4 (18)
VF-11	Essex	F2H-4 (12)
VF-22	Jacksonville	F2H-3 (8), F2H-4 (5)
VF-52	Bennington	F2H-3 (14)
VF-71	Key West	F2H-4 (16)
VF-92	Alameda	F2H-3 (19)
VF-121	Miramar	F2H-4 (2)
VF-124	Moffett	F2H-3 (4)
VF-152	Hornet	F2H-3 (10)
VF-194	Alameda	F2H-3 (1)
NAMTC	NAS Pt Mugu	F2H-3M (1)

FASRONS:
4	North Island	F2H-4 (2)
8	Alameda	F2H-3 (8), F2H-4 (6)
11	Atsugi	F2H-3 (3)
117	Barbers Pt.	F2H-4 (2)
119	Sangley Pt	F2H-3 (1)

31 MAY 1958
VFAW-4	Quonset Pt.	F2H-3 (9), F2H-4 (18)
VF-11	Essex	F2H-4 (12)
VF-22	Jacksonville	F2H-3 (7), F2H-4 (3)
VF-52	Bennington	F2H-3 (14)
VF-71	Key West	F2H-4 (17)
VF-92	Alameda	F2H-3 (19)
VF-121	Miramar	F2H-4 (2)
VF-124	Moffett	F2H-3 (1)
VF-152	Hornet	F2H-3 (10)
VF-194	Alameda	F2H-3 (1)
NAVCICOFFSCOL		F2H-3 (6)
NART	NAS Oakland	F2H-3 (6)

FASRONS:
4	North Island	F2H-4 (2)
6	Jacksonville	F2H-3 (3), F2H-4 (1)
8	Alameda	F2H-3 (8), F2H-4 (5)
9	Cecil	F2H-4 (1)
11	Atsugi	F2H-3 (3)
117	Barbers Pt.	F2H-4 (2)

30 JUN 1958
VFAW-4	Quonset Pt.	F2H-3 (11), F2H-4 (23)
VF-11	Essex	F2H-4 (12)
VF-52	Alameda	F2H-3 (14)
VF-71	Essex	F2H-4 (15)
VF-92	Alameda	F2H-3 (19)
VF-121	Miramar	F2H-4 (2)
VF-152	Hornet	F2H-3 (10)
VF-194	Alameda	F2H-3 (1)
NAVCICOFFSCOL		F2H-3 (16), F2H-4 (1)
NAS	North Island	F2H-3 (1)
NAF	Naples	F2H-4 (1)
NART	NAS Oakland	F2H-3 (7)

FASRONS:
4	North Island	F2H-4 (6)
6	Jacksonville	F2H-3 (1), F2H-4 (1)
8	Alameda	F2H-3 (10), F2H-4 (5)
9	Cecil	F2H-4 (1)
11	Atsugi	F2H-4 (2)

31 JUL 1958
VFAW-4	Quonset Pt.	F2H-4 (24), F2H-3 (8)
VF-11	Essex	F2H-4 (11)
VF-52	Ticonderoga	F2H-3 (12)
VF-71	Randolph	F2H-4 (8)
VF-92	Alameda	F2H-3 (9)
VF-121	Miramar	F2H-4 (2)
VF-152	Moffett	F2H-3 (12)
VF-194	Alameda	F2H-3 (1)
NAVCICOFFSCOL		F2H-3 (18), F2H-4 (3)
NART	NAS Oakland	F2H-3 (13)

FASRONS:
4	North Island	F2H-4 (11)
5	Oceana	F2H-4 (6)
6	Jacksonville	F2H-3 (1)
8	Alameda	F2H-4 (2), F2H-3 (13)
9	Cecil	F2H-4 (1)
11	Atsugi	F2H-3 (3)

31 AUG 1958
VFAW-4	Quonset Pt.	F2H-4 (24), F2H-3 (8)
VF-11	Essex	F2H-4 (11)
VF-52	Ticonderoga	F2H-3 (12)
VF-71	Randolph	F2H-4 (8)
VF-92	Alameda	F2H-3 (9)
VF-121	Miramar	F2H-4 (2)
VF-152	Moffett	F2H-3 (10)
VF-194	Alameda	F2H-3 (1)
NAVCICOFFSCOL		F2H-3 (23), F2H-4 (7)
NART	NAS Oakland	F2H-3 (14)

FASRONS:
4	North Island	F2H-4 (11)
5	Oceana	F2H-4 (7)
6	Jacksonville	F2H-3 (1)
8	Alameda	F2H-4 (2), F2H-3 (8)
9	Cecil	F2H-4 (1)
10	Moffett	F2H-3 (1)
11	Atsugi	F2H-3 (3)

30 SEP 1958
VFAW-4	Quonset Pt.	F2H-4 (25), F2H-3 (8)
VF-11	Essex	F2H-4 (11)
VF-52	Alameda	F2H-3 (13)
VF-71	Randolph	F2H-4 (8)
VF-92	Alameda	F2H-3 (9)
VF-152	Moffett	F2H-3 (10)
VF-194	Alameda	F2H-3 (1)
NAVCICOFFSCOL		F2H-3 (24), F2H-4 (10)
NART	NAS Oakland	F2H-3 (16)

FASRONS:
4	North Island	F2H-4 (10)
5	Oceana	F2H-4 (6)
6	Jacksonville	F2H-3 (1)
8	Alameda	F2H-3 (7)
9	Cecil	F2H-4 (1)
10	Moffett	F2H-3 (2)
11	Atsugi	F2H-3 (3)
104	Pt. Lyauty	F2H-4 (2)

31 OCT 1958
VFAW-4	Quonset Pt.	F2H-4 (24), F2H-3 (10)
VAW-11	North Island	F2H-4 (10)

VF-11 Essex F2H-4 (11)
VF-52 Ticonderoga F2H-3 (12)
VF-71 Randolph F2H-4 (8)
VF-92 Alameda F2H-3 (5), F3H-2 (9)
VF-92 Det N York. F2H-3 (4)
VF-152 Bennington F2H-3 (10)
NAVCICOFFSCOL F2H-3 (22), F2H-4 (19)
NART NAS Oakland F2H-3 (17)
FASRONS:
4 North Island F2H-4 (5)
5 Oceana F2H-4 (6)
6 Jacksonville F2H-3 (1)
8 Alameda F2H-3 (6)
10 Moffett F2H-3 (2)
11 Atsugi F2H-3 (3)
104 Pt. Lyauty F2H-4 (2)

30 NOV 1958
VFAW-4 Quonset Pt. F2H-4 (24), F2H-3 (6)
VAW-11 North Island F2H-4 (10)
VF-11 Jacksonville F2H-4 (11)
VF-52 Ticonderoga F2H-3 (12)
VF-71 Randolph F2H-4 (8)
VF-92 Alameda F2H-3 (5), F3H-2 (10)
VF-92 Det N York. F2H-3 (6)
VF-152 Bennington F2H-3 (10)
NAVCICOFFSCOL F2H-3 (24), F2H-4 (10)
NART NAS Oakland F2H-3 (18)
FASRONS:
4 North Island F2H-4 (5)
5 Oceana F2H-4 (6)
6 Jacksonville F2H-3 (1)
8 Alameda F2H-3 (5)
10 Moffett F2H-3 (1)
11 Atsugi F2H-3 (3)
104 Pt. Lyauty F2H-4 (2)

31 JAN 1959
VFAW-4 Quonset Pt. F2H-4 (29), F2H-3 (1)
VAW-11 North Island F2H-4 (10)
VF-11 Jacksonville F2H-4 (8)
VF-52 Ticonderoga F2H-3 (12)
VF-71 Randolph F2H-4 (7)
VF-92 Alameda F2H-3 (1), F3H-2 (12)
VF-92 Det N York. F2H-3 (4)
VF-152 Moffett F2H-3 (7)
NAVCICOFFSCOL F2H-3 (31), F2H-4 (10)
NART NAS Oakland F2H-3 (20)
FASRONS:
4 North Island F2H-4 (5)
5 Oceana F2H-4 (3)
6 Jacksonville F2H-3 (1)
8 Alameda F2H-3 (3)
10 Moffett F2H-3 (1)
11 Atsugi F2H-3 (2)

28 FEB 1959
VFAW-4 Quonset Pt. F2H-4 (29)
VAW-11 San Diego F2H-4 (9)
VF-71 Randolph F2H-4 (7)
VF-92 Det N York. F2H-4 (3)
VF-152 Moffett F2H-3 (3), ADs (12)
NAVCICOFFSCOL F2H-3 (35), F2H-4 (10)
NART NAS Oakland F2H-4 (1), F2H-3 (19)
FASRONS:
4 North Island F2H-4 (5)
5 Oceana F2H-4 (2)
6 Jacksonville F2H-3 (1)
8 Alameda F2H-3 (16)
10 Moffett F2H-3 (1)
11 Atsugi F2H-3 (11)

31 MAR 1959
VFAW-4 Quonset Pt. F2H-4 (29)
VAW-11 San Diego F2H-4 (7)
VF-92 Det N York. F2H-4 (3)

VF-152 Moffett F2H-3 (3), ADs (12)
NAVCICOFFSCOL F2H-3 (2), F2H-4 (12)
NART NAS Oakland F2H-4 (3), F2H-3 (23)
FASRONS:
3 Norfolk F2H-4 (2)
5 Oceana F2H-4 (2)
6 Jacksonville F2H-3 (1)
8 Alameda F2H-3 (7)
9 Cecil F2H-3 (1)
10 Moffett F2H-4 (1)
11 Atsugi F2H-4 (1)

30 APRIL 1959
VFAW-4 Quonset Pt. F2H-4 (27)
VAW-11 San Diego F2H-4 (7)
VF-92 Det N York. F2H-4 (5)
VF-152 Moffett F2H-3 (3), ADs (12)
NAVCICOFFSCOL F2H-3 (35), F2H-4 (12)
NARTU Norfolk F2H-4 (2)
NART NAS Oakland F2H-4 (3), F2H-3 (25)
FASRONS:
3 Norfolk F2H-4 (2)
4 North Island F2H-4 (2)
5 Oceana F2H-4 (2)
8 Alameda F2H-3 (4)
10 Moffett F2H-3 (1)

31 MAY 1959
VFAW-4 Quonset Pt. F2H-4 (24)
VAW-11 Det P Hornet F2H-3 (1), F2H-4 (4)
VF-92 Det N York. F2H-3 (3)
VF-152 Moffett F2H-3 (1), ADs (13)
NAVCICOFFSCOL F2H-3 (36), F2H-4 (12)
NARTU Norfolk F2H-4 (10)
NART NAS Oakland F2H-4 (3), F2H-3 (24)
FASRONS:
4 North Island F2H-3 (1)
8 Alameda F2H-3 (4)
10 Moffett F2H-3 (1)

30 JUN 1959
VFAW-4 Quonset Pt. F2H-4 (24)
VAW-11 Det P Hornet F2H-3 (1), F2H-4 (4)
NAVCICOFFSCOL F2H-3 (46), F2H-4 (12)
NARTU Norfolk F2H-4 (10)
NART NAS Oakland F2H-4 (3), F2H-3 (23)
FASRONS:
4 North Island F2H-3 (1)
8 Alameda F2H-3 (2)
10 Moffett F2H-3 (1)

31 JUL 1959
VAW-11 Det P Hornet F2H-3 (1), F2H-4 (4)
NAVCICOFFSCOL F2H-3 (44), F2H-4 (12)
NART Norfolk F2H-4 (10)
NART Oakland F2H-4 (23), F2H-3 (10)
FASRONS:
4 North Island F2H-3 (1)
10 Moffett F2H-3 (1)

31 AUG 1959
VU-2 Quonset F2H-4 (4)
VAW-11 Det P Hornet F2H-3 (1), F2H-4 (4)
NAVCICOFFSCOL F2H-3 (45)
NART Norfolk F2H-4 (10)
NART Oakland F2H-4 (29), F2H-3 (22)
FASRONS:
4 North Island F2H-3 (1)
10 Moffett F2H-3 (1)

30 SEP 1959
VU-2 Quonset F2H-4 (3)
VAW-11 Det P Hornet F2H-3 (1), F2H-4 (4)
NAVCICOFFSCOL F2H-3 (44)
NART Norfolk F2H-4 (10)
NART Oakland F2H-4 (28), F2H-3 (11)
FASRONS:
4 North Island F2H-3 (1)

30 NOV 1959
NAVCICOFFSCOL F2H-3 (42)
NART Norfolk F2H-4 (12)
NART Oakland F2H-4 (28), F2H-3 (12)

31 DEC 1959
NAVCICOFFSCOL F2H-3 (42)
NART Norfolk F2H-4 (12)
NART Oakland F2H-4 (28), F2H-3 (11)

31 JAN 1960
NAVCICOFFSCOL F2H-3 (41)
NART Norfolk F2H-4 (12)
NART Oakland F2H-4 (24), F2H-3 (10)

28 FEB 1960
NAVCICOFFSCOL F2H-3 (39)
NART Norfolk F2H-4 (12)
NART Oakland F2H-4 (24), F2H-3 (10)

31 MAR 1960
NAVCICOFFSCOL F2H-3 (35)
NART Norfolk F2H-4 (12)
NART Oakland F2H-4 (21), F2H-3 (9)

30 APR 1960
NAVCICOFFSCOL F2H-3 (34)
NART Norfolk F2H-4 (12)
NART Oakland F2H-4 (20), F2H-3 (9)

31 MAY1960
NAVCICOFFSCOL F2H-3 (28)
NART Norfolk F2H-4 (12)
NART Oakland F2H-4 (20), F2H-3 (9)

30 JUN 1960
NAVCICOFFSCOL F2H-3 (19)
NART Norfolk F2H-4 (12)
NART Oakland F2H-4 (19), F2H-3 (9)

31 JUL 1960
NAVCICOFFSCOL F2H-3 (14)
NART Norfolk F2H-4 (12)
NART Oakland F2H-4 (19), F2H-3 (9)

31 AUG 1960
NAVCICOFFSCOL F2H-3 (3)
NART Norfolk F2H-4 (10)
NART Oakland F2H-4 (19), F2H-3 (9)

30 SEP 1960
NART Norfolk F2H-4 (10)
NART Oakland F2H-4 (19), F2H-3 (9)

31 OCT 1960
NART Norfolk F2H-4 (10)
NART Oakland F2H-4 (19), F2H-3 (9)

30 NOV 1960
NART Norfolk F2H-4 (9)
NART Oakland F2H-4 (18), F2H-3 (9)

31 DEC 1960
NART Norfolk F2H-4 (9)
NART Oakland F2H-4 (15), F2H-3 (8)

31 JAN 1961
NART NAS Oakland F2H-4 (13), F2H-3 (7)

28 FEB 1961
NART NAS Oakland F2H-4 (1), F2H-3 (1)

ACADEMY/HOBBY CRAFT 1/72 SCALE F2H-3/4 BANSHEE

There have been numerous releases of the 1/72nd scale F2H-3/4 Banshee by Academy and Hobby Craft. The kit built below was Hobby craft kit#1356 offered with decals for VF-11 aircraft in either the gloss sea blue or gull grey and white scheme and Academy released kit#1626 with the same decals. Hobby Craft also released kit#1397 with Royal Canadian Navy box art and decals. The kit was a simple build but has one shortcoming. The main landing gear is not strong enough to support the model properly. The gear keeps bending outward and the rear fuselage needs to be supported by a piece of clear sprue to prevent this.

If you are going to build one of these, try to locate Skylancer decal sheet 7201 for markings of gull grey and white aircraft of VF-193, VA-152, VF-92, and VF-152 (mismarked as VF-151 on the decal sheet).

COLLECT AIRE 1/48 SCALE F2H-3/4 BANSHEE

The Collect Aire 1/48th scale multimedia (mostly resin) limited-run model kit was an excellent example of the Big Banjo as can be seen here in the built-up example of F2H-4 BuNo 127598 that was built by Fotis Rouch (via Collect Aire) with the markings of VF-11 as supplied with the kit. The kit included decals for two US (VF-11 and VF-194) and two Canadian aircraft.

VACUFORM 1/72 SCALE F2H-3/4 BANSHEE KIT BY EXECUFORM

The Execuform 1/72nd scale kit of the F2H-3/4 Banshee dates back to the early days of vacuform. This 1970's kit was crude by today's standards and suffers from one of my first attempts at building a vacuform kit. I did not sand down the flying surfaces sufficiently and the resulting thick flying surfaces make the model look horsey and the kit less accurate than it actually was.

The kit contained no decals and no detail parts and certainly is not worth the effort to find and build since the Hobby Craft and Academy kits were released.

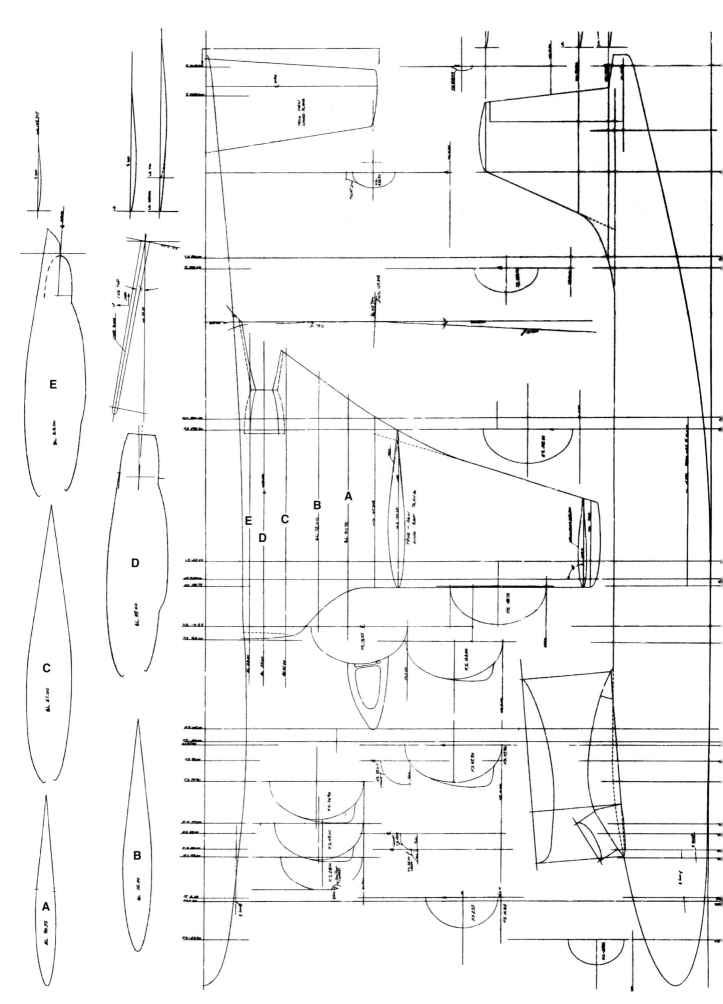